UNDER ONE CANOPY

Readings
in
Jewish Diversity

About the Publisher

Kulanu was established as a tax-exempt 501(c)(3) organization in 1994 to assist lost and dispersed Jewish communities around the world. It maintains a web site at <www.Kulanu.org>.

In 1998, Kulanu published the hardcover book *Jews in Places You Never Thought Of* jointly with KTAV Publishing House. Also edited by Karen Primack, that book is a compilation of 45 authors' reports about largely unknown Jewish communities, including the Bnei Menashe in northeastern India, the Abayudaya Jews of Uganda, the Kaifeng Jewish community of China, descendants of Iberian Crypto-Jews around the world, and groups in Peru and Ghana.

Kulanu also produced *Shalom Everybody Everywhere*, a popular commercial-quality recording of Ugandan-Jewish music, in 1997. The organization publishes a quarterly newsletter and operates e-mail discussion groups in English and Spanish. It operates an online boutique <www.KulanuBoutique.com> that offers books, recordings, and international handicrafts.

Kulanu programs include assistance to Jewish schools and religious institutions in developing countries, modest stipends for teachers to work in these communities, the shipping of Jewish books and ritual items, and more.

Kulanu fosters mutually beneficial interactions between mainstream Jews and these isolated communities. The organization emphasizes networking with and traveling to the developing Jewish communities. Kulanu also educates mainstream Jews about these groups, which we "discover" regularly.

This book is a tribute to Jewish diversity by Sephardi, Ashkenzai, Mizrahi, African, and Asian writers. Proceeds will benefit Kulanu's programs.

UNDER ONE CANOPY
Readings in Jewish Diversity

Edited by
Karen Primack

KULANU
"All of Us"

Published by Kulanu, Inc.

Library of Congress Control Number: 2003097622
ISBN: 0-9746104-0-2

Printed in The United States of America by
Network Printers, Inc.
1010 70th Street
Milwaukee, WI 53214

Table of Contents

MODERN ISRAEL

ALL OF US

*   Prize winners, 2002 Kulanu International Writing Competition
** Songs

Introduction

Contrary to the belief of some, the Jews are a multiracial, multi-ethnic group. But it should not be surprising that Judaism's 4000-year-old creed spans geography as well as time, or that its message appeals to members of all races, on all continents. This diversity of the Jewish population is cause for celebration.

These selections will introduce the reader to a wonderful array of Jews of varied backgrounds. Sephardi, Ashkenazi, and Mizrachi Jews are represented. The continents of Africa and Asia are singled out. Jews by Choice are here, and a special niche for the Jews of modern Israel. We've organized our selections within these categories—to emphasize the range of places and events that shape Jews' identities. These categories are not so neat and often overlap—but that's the point, isn't it?

We hasten to add that these selections and categories are not exhaustive. Similarly, the weight some groups appear to have in this volume is not indicative of their importance in the Jewish scheme of things. We are limited by the entries we received, as well as the sources with which we are familiar. We hope that the unrepresented and under-represented groups will be heard from in future volumes.

I was inspired to compile this book at a Diversity Shabbat at my synagogue (Tifereth Israel in Washington, DC), which featured a number of readings by or about Jews from different cultures. Kulanu offers this volume as a source for synagogue services, home ceremonies, communal gatherings, and quiet contemplation of the rich diversity to be found within Judaism.

Why is Jewish diversity cause for celebration?

A happy reason to celebrate Jewish diversity is the opportunity it gives Jews to use and appreciate the variety of liturgy, literature, music, food, customs, and personalities. Congregations and individuals can choose from a wide array to enrich—but not necessarily replace—their own practices.

Another reason, a sad one, is that we may need each other. History teaches us that a Jew never knows when he will need help, or where that help might come from. Ibo attorney Remy Ilona, a practicing Jew in Abuja, Nigeria, has written on the need for all Jewish peoples to speak out and write about problems such as the demonization of Israel by academia and violent acts of anti-Semitism in Europe: "If a Lemba, an Ethiopian Jew, an Abayudaya, an Ibo, a Honduran Jew, etc., all get articles into papers calling for world sympathy for Israel, I believe the world will begin to realize the truth [that Israel has been unfairly victimized]." Indeed, one is reminded of an article in a Praetoria paper (*The Citizen Newspaper* of 5 September 2001) reporting that the Lemba (a black South African community with Jewish roots) defended Israel against charges that "Zionism is racism" at the UN conference on racism in Durban.

Another benefit we derive from being aware of our diverse cousins is that we are reminded of how valuable our religious heritage is. After all, why else would it have so much global appeal—without forced conversions or even proselytizing?

We have adopted the canopy as our symbol of inclusiveness. We are conceiving of a metaphorical covering over the Jewish people—all of it. A general reader may think of a canopy as a canvas overhead covering protecting outdoor diners at a restaurant. An environmentalist might think of a forest canopy, the treetop cover that lets in just the right amount of light and water to protect the ecosystems within it and below it. A Jew may think of a *huppah*, or wedding canopy, such as the one pictured on our cover. The *huppah* traditionally represents the home the bride and groom will create together.

A canopy is a covering that protects and connects those under it. As it is metaphorical, our canopy can stretch to any size we desire—open enough to let in all who wish to come and cozy enough to unite us.

Karen Primack
October 2003

ACKNOWLEDGEMENTS

The lion's share of credit goes to these wonderful 50 writers and composers, who state the case for diversity so eloquently. Helping me in my compilation and editing roles were Dr. Judy Neri, Aaron Nagar, Dr. Yohannes Zeleke, Gretchen Primack, Dr. Maureen Goldsmith, and, most of all, Dr. Aron Primack, my helpmate. Poet Jean Nordhaus served as the distinguished judge of the 2002 Kulanu International Writing Competition (the winning pieces are included in this book). The cover design is by graphic artist Avrum Ashery, who also designed the Kulanu logo.

Meet the Contributors

Rabbi Barbara Aiello has been the spiritual leader of Temple Beth El in Bradenton, Florida, for four years. Prior to her ordination from Rabbinical Seminary International in New York City, she was a teacher, counselor and professional puppeteer. She is the creator of The Kids on the Block puppets, used around the world to help children understand and accept differences and disabilities, and in 1989 won the Surgeon General's Medallion for Excellence in Public Health. In 2001 Rabbi Aiello was awarded an advanced *s'micha* from the Rabbinical Seminary for her work in community outreach. She is the host of her own radio program on Jewish themes, "The Radio Rabbi," heard every Sunday morning on WLSS-AM 930 in Sarasota. Rabbi Aiello serves the Anousim community by helping Italian and Spanish families who have Jewish ancestry return to their Jewish roots.

Avrum Ashery (cover and logo designer), a nationally known Judaic artist, graphic designer, educator and lecturer, has created logos, national posters, Judaic fine arts, and stained glass windows for over 30 years. He is the former art director of Walter Reed Medical Center and of the National Institute of Mental Health.

Robin Becker is the author of five collections of poems including *The Horse Fair* (University of Pittsburgh Press, 2000) and *All-American Girl* (University of Pittsburgh Press, 1996), for which she won the Lambda Literary Award in Lesbian Poetry. A professor of English and Women's Studies at the Pennsylvania State University, she serves as poetry editor for *The Women's Review of Books*, a publication of the Wellesley College Center for Research on Women.

Born and raised in Haifa, Israel, **Dahlia Blech** has lived with her family in California since 1984. A student of piano from age 7, she always loved playing by ear, especially Israeli folk songs. She has led and accompanied monthly Israeli sing-along evenings for more than 14 years, and has been part of the musical group Side by Side since its formation in 1996. This group consists of six Jewish mothers and grandmothers who write, arrange and perform their own original music and lyrics. Side by Side has produced two CDs of their original songs: *Arise and Shine* and *On Wings of Song*

French-born **Ilan Braun** lives in a very small village in Morbihan, southern Brittany. He writes a monthly column on nature in Israel for the largest French Jewish magazine *L'Arche* (*The Ark*). He lived in Israel for two years; Israel is central to his activities, which include, besides poetry, art (several book covers), wildlife conservation, and research on Jewish war refugees in Brittany. He has travelled widely, from Australia to India, via Iran and Afghanistan, and participated in two ecology workshops in the US with a grant from National Audubon Society.

Rose Bromberg writes poetry, prose, and short stories. She is facilitator of the creative writing class and editor of *Horizons Magazine* at the Riverdale Senior Center, as well as book coordinator for Kulanu. She enjoys reading novels and poetry on the Middle East and the Orient, and is working on a project involving poetry and photography.

Rabbi Angela Warnick Buchdahl completed both her cantorial and rabbinical studies at Hebrew Union College in New York, where she was a Wexner Graduate Fellow. She serves Westchester Reform Temple in Scarsdale, New York.

Mishael Maswari Caspi was born in Israel to Yemenite Jewish parents. He is the author of numerous books and articles on the creative works of Jews in the Islamic world.

His compilation of poetry, *Daughters of Yemen* (University of California Press 1985), is the result of extensive fieldwork in Yemenite Jewish communities throughout Israel.

Born and raised in Brazil, **Clara Castelar** has been living in Shepherdstown, West Virginia, for the past 30 years. A freelance writer, artist and jewelry maker, she is currently working on a novel based on her Sephardic family history. Her strong interest in genealogy began at age 29, when she discovered that she is descended from Spanish and Portuguese Crypto-Jews who had settled in Brazil in the 16th century.

Norman Chansky is a professor *emeritus* at Temple University, where he taught psychology for many years, and was a visiting professor at Tel Aviv University 1973-1974. Several of his poems have appeared in *Jewish Currents*, one of which, "A Tribute to Anton Schmid" (a righteous gentile), was set to music by Pete Seeger. He is currently completing a book of verse called *Soul of My People*, which begins at creation and ends at the present.

Retirees **Jerry and Jocelyn Cooper** live in Canada and winter in Florida. They both play guitar and sing in English, French, Hebrew and Ladino, but their passion is Yiddish music. They also write songs and frequently lead sing-alongs, including at Kulanu gatherings in Southern Florida.

Rachel S. Epstein is 22 years old and a recent graduate of Binghamton University. She has published work in *Newsday, The New York Times*, and the *Chicago Tribune*. A Long Island native, she plans to attend an MFA program.

Stuart Federow has been the rabbi of Congregation Shaar Hashalom in Houston, Texas, since 1989. He can be reached at <stuartfederow@hotmail.com>. He developed <www.whatjewsbelieve.org>, a web site with information to help Jews respond to Christian missionaries.

Born in England, **Ruth Fogelman** came to Jerusalem as a teenager. She served in the IDF and received her degree in English Literature from the Hebrew University. She has lived in the Jewish Quarter of Jerusalem for the last 23 years. She photographs, writes and lectures about the Jewish Quarter. Her poems, articles and photographs have been published by numerous journals, and she has designed a line of greeting cards. Her book, *Within the Walls of Jerusalem*, about present-day life in the Jewish Quarter, was recently released.

Michael Freund served as Deputy Director of Communications and Policy Planning under former Israeli Prime Minister Benjamin Netanyahu. He is currently the Director of Amishav, a Jerusalem-based organization which reaches out and assists "lost Jews" seeking to return to the Jewish people.

Stephen L. Gomes is a professor of international business at California State University at Northridge and Oregon Health and Science University in Portland. He is also founding partner of Gomes and Company, a small boutique consulting practice specializing in international strategic alliances, joint ventures, corporate matchmaking and business mediation He received his Ph.D. in 1976 from the University of Pittsburgh in Public and International Management. In his younger days, he served with the Peace Corps in Brazil.

Canada-born **Gila Green** received Journalism and English Literature degrees in Ottawa and moved to Israel in 1994. Now a freelance writer and editor, she lives in Ramat Beit Shemesh with her three small children.

Schulamith Chava Halevy writes poetry in Hebrew and English. Born to a Sephardic family whose ancestors were exiled from Spain, Halevy has dedicated herself to researching the heritage of contemporary *Anousim*, the crypto-Jewish descendents of the forced converts of 15th-century Spain and Portugal. She has been documenting their survival and studying the nature of their identity. Halevy is a doctoral candidate at Hebrew University; her dissertation is on the *Anousim* in Mexico.

Hadassah W. Harr-Ell, a wife, mother, grandmother, scriptwriter, poet, free-lance writer, certified secretary, certified home health aide and holistic healer, grew up in Harlem, New York City, in a hidden (Sephardi/Ethiopian Jewish) environment, where she had to avoid exposing her Jewishness. She now lives in Beth Shemesh, Israel, where she and her husband work on scripts, poetry and writings about Jewish Diversity <http://www.geocities.com/teamscriptwriters/index.html>. She is secretary-general of SE'ATA, a new website in Jerusalem founded by women of African descent.

Max Amichai Heppner, who is married and has four children and nine grandchildren in his blended family, retired from the U.S. Department of Agriculture as a public information officer in 1994. He has produced a documentary about his experiences as a hidden child during the Holocaust and is writing two books based on these experiences, one of them for children. He is Kulanu's Regional Coordinator for Mexico, interested in resurfacing *Anousim*. He has recently taken training as a mediator to resolve disputes outside of the court system. He is a member of the Jewish Renewal movement.

Carolivia Herron teaches creative writing at the College of William and Mary, Virginia, and at Montgomery College, Maryland, and has held professorial appointments at Harvard University and Mount Holyoke College. She directs PAUSE (Potomac Anacostia Ultimate Story Exchange), an e-mail creative writing mentoring program in Washington, DC, where she has also taught recently at the Children's Studio School Charter School. She holds a Ph.D. in Comparative Literature from the University of Pennsylvania in the area of European and African epic. Her numerous publications include the controversial children's book *Nappy Hair* and the novel *Thereafter Johnnie*.

Sarajevo-born **Flory Jagoda** performs traditional and original compositions of Sephardic songs. Recipient of a 2002 National Endowment for the Arts National Heritage Fellowship, she has also been named a Master Artist in the Folklife Apprenticeship Program at the Virginia Foundation for the Humanities. Jagoda gives lectures and concerts worldwide as a solo artist and also with her family musical group. She has produced four recordings, and a documentary about her life, *The Key From Spain*, has been featured in film festivals.

W. Luther Jett is the author of a chapbook of poems and original graphics, *A Leather Dress Fur Mother*. His poems have also appeared in numerous journals. His own website, a multi-media exploration of the Hyper-text medium, can be found at <http://members.aol.com/magendror/freebird/entrance.htm>. A member of Adat Shalom Reconstructionist Congregation in Bethesda, Maryland, he was raised in a Protestant family and came to Judaism after a long spiritual and philosophical journey. He notes, "I think it all started when I was around nine or ten years old and my mother started bringing home Challah from the Giant supermarket every weekend. One of my sisters also converted to Judaism."

Kokasi Keki, a member of the Abayudaya Jews of Uganda, lives near Mbale, Uganda, with his parents and two sisters. He wrote "Jewish in Africa" in 2002, when he was 11 years old and in P5 (fifth grade in primary school). His father, Aaron Kintu Moses, is an Abayudaya leader who, upon graduating from Makere University, founded the Hadassah Infant School. Kokasi Keki's mother, Naome Sabano, is president of the Abayudaya Women's Association.

Yitzchak Kerem is a historian and researcher on Greek and Sephardic Jewry at Aristotle University in Thessaloniki, Greece, and at Hebrew University of Jerusalem. He is founder and director of the Institute of Hellenic-Jewish Relations at the University of Denver (Colorado), and has been editor of the monthly academic e-mail publication *Sefarad* since 1992. He is a board member of Casa Shalom and co-founder of the International Forum for Tolerance and Peace.

Loolwa Khazzoom <http://www.loolwa.com> is the director of the Jewish MultiCultural Project and editor of *The Flying Camel: Essays on Identity by Women of North African and Middle Eastern Jewish Heritage* (Seal Press, Winter 2003). She has published Jewish multicultural articles in numerous periodicals, including *The Washington Post. Rolling Stone,* and *Marie Claire*

Romanian-born **Emma Kimor** is an Israeli who writes, translates, gives readings and lectures in English, Hebrew and German. A former poetry editor and holder of several prestigious literary awards, she is married to an internationally eminent marine biologist, with whom she has traveled in many parts of the world. She is working on two books (a travel volume and an historic memoir) and has three complete works, waiting for a publisher—a poetry book called *Wings*, a collection of wit and anecdotes called *Chuckles*, and her thoughts on three major wars in Israel as told by the mother of a soldier, entitled *A Woman Asks Why?*

A recent graduate of Yale University, **Margie Klein** spent last year on the Green Corps fellowship, where she led grassroots organizing campaigns on clean air and forest issues for the Sierra Club, Florida PIRG, and GreenpeaceUSA. Now she works for the Center for Health, Environment, and Justice as an organizer on children's environmental health issues. As an observant Jew, Margie derives much of her sense of social and environmental responsibility from the Jewish tradition. She recently organized the Adam V'Adamah conference, which worked to harness the power of the Jewish community to promote clean energy for the planet and Israel.

Rabbi Benjamin Z. Kreitman was born in Warsaw, Poland, and grew up in Louisville, Kentucky. He studied at Yale and Yeshiva Universities and was ordained by the Jewish Theological Seminary of America. He was the first rabbi to serve on the New York City Board of Health; he was also chairman of the Brooklyn Commission on Human Rights and Equal Opportunity and chairman of the Brooklyn Small Business Opportunities Corporation. He has served as chairman of the Rabbinical Assembly's Committee on Jewish Law and Standards, and in 1976-1989 was the executive vice-president of the United Synagogue of America. He is currently executive vice-president *emeritus*; Rabbi of the World Council of Conservative/ Masorti Synagogues; and vice-chairman of MERCAZ (the Zionist Organization of the Conservative Movement). Rabbi Kreitman has written extensively on Jewish law, theology, the Musar Movement and on Homiletics in the modern pulpit.

Robin K. Levinson is an award-winning journalist, Web editor, and author whose articles appear in *Jewish Woman Magazine*. She also writes book reviews for *Jewish Book World.* She lives with her daughter, Zoe, 10; son, Aaron, 8; and her husband, Larry, in Hamilton, New Jersey.

American-born **Lori Levy** lived in Israel for 16 years, and now resides in Los Angeles with her husband and three children. Her poems have appeared in a variety of literary journals as well as in medical and health-related journals. Her writing has also appeared or is forthcoming in various Jewish journals, such as *Jewish Women's Literary Annual*, *Bridges, Jewish Affairs* (in South Africa), *Voices Israel*, and *Moznaim* (in Hebrew translation).

Rufina Bernardetti Silva Mausenbaum, poet, artist and writer, is founder of <www.saudades.org>, a web-site serving Sephardim and Bnei Anousim with Portuguese

ancestry. An *Anous* from Portugal and Madeira , she also founded the Saudades-Sefarad Forum at < http://groups.yahoo.com/group/saudades-sefarad/>. She returned to Judaism in the Orthodox tradition. She resides in Johannesburg, South Africa, and is director of Root and Branch Ibereo-Israel Fellowship, Kulanu liaison for Portugal, and an active member of The Association for Fair Media S.A.

Gloria Mound is executive director of the Institute for Marrano (Anusim) Studies, an organization she founded 30 years ago in Israel. In 1985 she relocated temporarily to Ibiza to study the secret synagogues first-hand, and discovered a 15th-century Megilla Esther. Her research expanded to other areas of Spain. She is an Honorary Research Fellow of Glasgow University and gives lecture tours in the US and Europe regularly. Her institute <www.casa-shalom.com> helps modern-day *Anousim* from all continents and has developed an impressive library of source materials.

Judy Neri, a Kulanu activist, is a prize-winning Maryland poet and writer/editor with a Ph.D. in Comparative Literature. Her poems appear in numerous journals and books, and she has given readings and talks on poetry and women's music.. Her sonnet "Teen Lovers" was read by Garrison Keillor on National Public Radio's *Writer's Almanac.* "Psalm of Questions" was published in *Covenant of the Soul* by Women of Reform Judaism in 2000. She is at work on a chapbook whose working title is *The Why of It.*

Karen Primack, a Kulanu Board member, edited *Jews in Places You Never Thought Of* (KTAV 1998) and produced *Shalom Everybody Everywhere*, a commercial CD of Ugandan-Jewish music. She has edited the Kulanu newsletter for ten years. Avid travelers, she and her husband have visited over 50 countries and have lived in Uganda and Niger.

Marjorie Stamm Rosenfeld's career history includes a stint as Manuscript Editor for the Southern Methodist University Press, seven years of teaching in the SMU English Department, over 13 years as a Navy analyst in the TRIDENT Missile Program, and bibliotherapy with the criminally insane as a volunteer in a mental hospital. Now a volunteer with Jewishgen, she has created three web sites on perished Jewish communities in Eastern Europe. Some of her poems can be found on the Internet as well as in various literary journals and anthologies.

Isabelle Medina Sandoval is an assistant professor at the College of Santa Fe and teaches literacy and education classes. Her passions include writing and researching New Mexico history, water rights, land grants, and Crypto-Jewish research. Some of her poetry is included in *Another Desert* by Sherman and Asher. She is a member of Hadassah and a board member for the New Mexico Jewish Historical Society. She is included in *Who's Who in America, 2004*, and *Who's Who in the World, 2004.*

Lynn Schubert grew up in Syracuse, NY, and Phoenix, Arizona. With Masters Degrees in education curriculum and in English, she has taught all levels, including English Composition at Harbor College in California, where she now resides. She is the author of *Song of Eli's Child*, an anthology of her poetry, and is working on a novel. She is married and has four children and seven grandchildren.

Rachel Ziona Segal is currently a happy grandmother in Huntington, NY. Born in Panama to a Persian-born father and Hebron-born mother, she grew up as an Orthodox Jew attending a Catholic school. She served as education director of the Dix Hills Jewish Center Religious school for 20 years, and now volunteers at a senior citizen home.

Murray F. Siegel and **Rickey Stein** have worked dozens of years on a collection of translations of the *Ma Nishtana* from around the world. Murray has created a variety of novel seder experiences over a period of 30 years, some of which are on a web site he developed at http://sedersforyou.tripod.com.

Gershom Sizomu is the spiritual leader of the Abayudaya Jews of Uganda. He founded the Semei Kakungulu High School, Uganda's only Jewish parochial high school. He is an accomplished singer, musician, and songwriter. He is currently studying for rabbinic ordination at the University of Judaism in Los Angeles.

Rosalie Sogolow began her musical career writing musical plays for her classes to perform as a teacher in the Chicago public schools. In 1987 she began teaching English to elderly Russian immigrants; their oral histories and recipes became the basis for her first book, *Memories from a Russian Kitchen: From Shtetl to Golden Land.* Her award-winning second book, *Empty the Ocean with a Spoon,* is a cornucopia of Jewish culture, Yiddish expressions and family traditions. She performs with Dahlia Blech in the musical group Side by Side.

Elaine Starkman is a San Francisco-area writer of prose and poetry who once lived in Israel. She wrote *Learning to Sit in the Silence: A Journal of Caretaking,* and edited the award-winning *Here I Am: Contemporary Jewish Stories from Around the World.* She is currently working on her fifth chapbook of poems, *MOVING: Poems 1992-2002.* Her other works can be found in *Family: A View from the Interior, The Use of Narrative in the Helping Professions,* and numerous books and journals. Having taught in a college setting for 15 years, she now works with mature adults on their memoirs.

Lucy Y. Steinitz, Ph.D. was executive director of Jewish Family Services of Central Maryland for 15 years, until 1997. That year, she and her family moved to Windhoek Namibia, where—together with a Catholic missionary doctor—she co-founded Catholic AIDS Action. She currently works as that organization's national coordinator. She also co-founded and chairs the Board of Trustees of Namibia's interfaith Church Alliance for Orphans, and she is vice-president of Namibia's only synagogue, the Windhoek Hebrew Congregation.

The author of 20 books of poetry and fiction, **Herman Taube** was born in Lodz, Poland, in 1918. During World War II, he lived as an exile in Uzbekestan and was stationed in Majdanek, where he served as a medic in the Second Polish Army. He participated in the liberation of Poland and administered medical care to those who survived the camps. In 1947, he immigrated to America with his wife Susan Taube. He has been a frequent contributor to the *Yiddish Forward.*

Sue Tourkin-Komet was born and raised in the Washington, DC, area and immigrated to Jerusalem at age 19, in 1968. She is a licensed social worker, journalist, freelance writer, proud mother of one grown-up special daughter, a sometimes artist, and a sometimes matchmaker. Her poetry and prose have been published in about a dozen English-language publications in Israel, the US, Canada, and England. She has done poetry performances in Jerusalem and New York City.

Paul Wieder has been a writer for the Jewish Federation of Chicago since 1995. He became the "Jewish Jukebox" columnist for the online magazine *Jewish World Review* in 2000 and has been publishing articles on Jewish music and musicians for Chicago's *JUF News* since 1996. His song "A Little Help is All I Need" is featured on the 1998 award-winning album *Color Me Singing* by Susan Salidor, and his comedic sketches have appeared on Chicago television. He is currently at work on two musicals.

Rabbi J. Hershy Worch was born in Manchester, England, and was ordained in 1992 by Rabbi Shlomo Carlebach. He has served in pulpits and with campus Hillel groups in the US and Australia. In 1996 he lived with and taught the Abayudaya at Nabugoye Hill near Mbale, Uganda. He is an artist, musician, dramatist and poet. His book *Sacred Fire, Torah from the Years of Fury 1939-43,* a translation of the Hebrew manuscript authored by R. Kalonymos Kalmish Shapira, Rebbe of the Warsaw Ghetto, was published by Jason Aronson in 2000. His new book *The Kabbalist Haggadah: A Handbook of the Seder* is coming out soon.

Xu Xin, professor of History of Jewish Culture and director of the Center for Jewish Studies at Nanjing University, is also president of the China Judaic Studies Association and editor-in-chief and a major contributor of the Chinese edition of *Encyclopedia Judaica*. In 2003 he was awarded an honorary doctorate by Bar Ilan University in recognition of the extremely important work he has done on research of the Jewish people in China.

Eva Rita (Schultz) Yelloz, born in a Displaced Persons Camp in Eschwege, Germany, of Polish Holocaust-surviving parents, was raised in New York. She currently resides in Sherman Oaks, California, where she operates her own public relations business geared to the Jewish community. She has been extensively published in Los Angeles-based Jewish newspapers and is currently working on her first novel, about an *agunah* (a "chained woman" without an official religious divorce document).

Sephardim/Anousim

"Sephardim" are Jews of Spanish origin.

"Anousim" (Hebrew for "forced ones") were the Spanish and Portuguese Jews who converted to Christianity under duress during the 15ᵗʰ and 16ᵗʰ centuries. Some of them, the Crypto-Jews, converted outwardly but continued to practice Judaism secretly, often at great personal risk.

"Bnai Anousim" are the descendants of these forced converts.

"Marrano" is a pejorative term referring to an Anous or Crypto-Jew.

Sefarad, 1492*

W. Luther Jett

The oak-trees are sighing;
    how their leaves fall, like the tears
    of a young girl,
who is longing for her lover—
He has gone to be a sailor.

The wind blows from the hills, down
    through the bright, deserted valleys.
Where has everybody vanished to—
    Everybody who once lived here?

Above the western city-gate
    is a room where I once lay
    in my love's arms;
now the dust blows in the window,
and my lover's arms lie empty.

The moonlight casts no shadows
    where the highway crosses over
a river filled with teardrops
    that is always overflowing.

The oak-trees are praying;
    how they lift their naked
    limbs to heaven—
Who will hear their lamentations?
None are living that might answer.

The white storks are flying;
    how their wings gleam over the ocean,
and the sailors, in the morning,
    hear them crying for lost summers.

* First Prize Winner, 2002 Kulanu International Writing Competition

Medina Frontier*

Isabelle Medina Sandoval

Midnight

O Crescent Moon
crying in the marble darkness
in blessed cross *relajando* opportune

I hear the thunder
of swords slicing in Granada
and women sobbing in the *almuada*

O Allah Moon
Where is your jasmine perfume

I wrap my lace mantilla
in these *tierras ajenas de Castilla*
and my heart thinks this prayer *sencilla*

Eterno ame la morada de tu casa
con este Torquemada que me pasa

Half Past Midnight

Earth water wind and fire
Will I see light in this mire

Again I leave another country in exile
Have I strength to travel another mile

And the wind sings another old song
in the soulful Arabic al ud long gone
Ay ay ay ay ay Ay ay ay ay ay

One a.m.

O Pyramid Moon
waning in the silver emptiness
of rosary and *quetzalcuatl* monsoon

22

I see the fires
of pyres in Mexico City
and bodies burning without pity

O *Nahuatl* Moon
Where is your rose water perfume

I wrap my Spanish silk *rebozo*
in the desolate desert so *enfintoso*
and my mind speaks this prayer *doloroso*

De generacion en generacion se alba tu obra
as our unborn children sing praises in diaspora

Half Past One

Earth water wind and fire
I need light as I transpire

Again I leave another desert in exile
Can I commute for just one more mile

And the wind sings another old song
in a flaming flamenco guitar long gone
Ay ay ay ay ay Ay ay ay ay ay

Two a.m.

I toss and turn and cannot sleep
I dream of the familiar *Calabaza* Moon
while sitting under the olive trees and weep
on red rock hills for melodies of a forgotten tune

Why why why I wonder in my *cabeza*
there must be some meaning to my *bajeza*

Half Past Two

I move to the edge of my *camalta*

and open the corner of my *maleta*

And what is that *criatura* in my window I see
but a ghost of *San Gabriel* of our ancestral tree

And again I leave another dream in exile
while wandering on sands of the Nile

And the wind sings an old song
in the soulful Hibr lyre long gone
Ay ay ay ay ay Ay ay ay ay ay

Three a.m.

O Ecliptic Moon
lost in velvety hollowness
to *mishpaha* now universally strewn

I feel my heart
gyrating to my secret nation
frozen in halachic consecration

Half Past Three

O Apache Moon
shining in snowy bloodiness
to whispers of ghosts as they croon

I observe the ways
of our isolated people
incongruent with saintly steeple

O Native Moon
where is your piñon perfume

I knot my bandana
in this lovely Mora montaña
thinking of the Americano mañana

El Señor lives en *la morada*

in the mortar of *gente olvidada*

Four a.m.

Earth water wind and fire
Will I see light you inspire

Again I leave a county in exile
trying to make *feria* in US style

The wind sings the *cante jondo* song
of a *pitero's* hidden soul almost gone
Ay ay ay ay ay Ay ay ay ay ay

Dawn

Earth water wind and fire
there is the light I desire

And the wind sings a new song
of soulful ud lyre guitar and flute
of red first fruit made from clay root
Ay ay ay ay ay Ay ay ay ay ay

As far as east is from the west
the west is east sun in my breast

O Cryptic Moon
hiding in exiled wilderness
I smell your Hadassah perfume

Jubilee Times Tithe

Shards of reality light
in the moonbeams swim
in mystical millennial twilight
illuminating the secluded *Ivrim*

In the new day I comprehend
Arab brick to Pueblo mud does transcend

linking the Levant red clay to Iberian blend
and cohabiting with others as spiritual friend

Earthly hand
watered by a Rio Grande
fired by the tiny moonbeam
and spirited by breath of Elohim

Abra ca dabra
I am the *Ivri sabra*
the prickly pear cactus flower
crossing Israeli borders by higher power

Oh Oh *Anousi* Moon
I smell your *shoshanah* perfume

Ay ay ay ay ay ay ay ay ay ay
Ay ay ay ay ay ay ay ay ay ay

In the warm *hesed*
of Hashem's *merced*
in my borderless *medinat*
my *neshama* praises *shabat*

*Second Prize Winner, 2002 Kulanu International Writing Competition

Author's Note:
The realistic dream chronicles the abrupt midnight 1492 expulsion of Jews from Spain terminating the *convivencia* in Spain, to escaping to Mexico to find the Mexican Inquisition seeking *conversos*. At two a.m. the collective memory of living in Yisrael stirs the soul and I wake up with the realization that my ancestors in San Gabriel also journeyed the same exile in Egypt. At three o'clock I come to the realization that I have survived in New Mexico but know I must keep this secret because of the long arm of the Mexican Inquisition still searching for heresy and *conversos*. At three-thirty, I find myself in the forests of the Sangre de Cristo wondering why the family customs do not parallel Native American and Catholic ways. At four a.m., I hear the soulful Semitic music of the Penitent in the cactus and pine mountains and at dawn I realize that the Crypto-Jewish experience lives in my heart. In Jubilee Times Tithe, 50 times 10, or 500 years later, I wake up to the realization that the New Mexican journey constitutes a synergy of Native American, Arab and Jewish factors protected by Hashem to survive the Iberian Inquisition and explusion. At last I know I can openly practice my faith near the Rio Grande of the Southwest.

Glossary

relajando – New Mexico term used for expressing public shame

almuada – New Mexico term for pillow; Spanish-*almodada*; Ladino-*almoada*

tierras ajenas de Castilla – foreign lands of Castilla, Spain

sencilla – (Sp.) simple

Eterno ame la morada de tu casa – (Sp.) Eternal One, I loved the dwelling of your house

con este Torquemada que me pasa – (Sp.) With this Torquemada, what will happen to me?

Quetzalcuatl – Nahuatl word for green feather of a bird

Nahuatl – Aztec language of Mexico

rebozo – (Sp.) shawl or covering

enfintoso – (Sp.) deceitful

doloroso – (Sp.) sorrowful

De generacion en generacion se alba tu obra – (Sp.) From generation to generation Your work will be praised

Calabaza – (Sp.) pumpkin; Ladino-*kalavasa*

cabeza – (Sp.) head; Ladino-*kavesa*

bajeza – (Sp.) weakness

camalta – Colonial New Mexico Spanish for *cama alta*, high bed; Hebrew-*kama;* Ladino-*kama*

maleta – (Sp.) valise; Hebrew-*malat*

criatura – (Sp.) child; Ladino-*kriatura*

San Gabriel – first Spanish capital of New Mexico, started in 1598

Mora – town of 1835 Mora Land Grant in New Mexico

montana – (Sp.) mountain; Ladino-*montanya*

El Señor – (Sp.) The Man or The Eternal One

la morada – (Sp.) the dwelling place or habitation; Ladino-*morada*

gente olvidada – (Sp.) the forgotten people

feria – New Mexico Spanish, money or change once traded at fairs; Ladino-f*erya*

cante jondo – Semitic lamenting music of Andalucia

pitero's – New Mexico Spanish for penitent flute player's

Rio Grande – (Sp.) Great River, located in New Mexico

sabra – Hebrew term for prickly and tough on the outside while sweet inside as the prickly pear cactus, a native plant of the American Southwest and Mexico transplanted in Israel; also, an Israeli-born Jew

Anousi – (Heb.) forced convert, term for descendants of Iberian Peninsula

hesed – (Heb.) loving kindness

merced – (Sp.) gift; Ladino-*mersed*

medinat – (Heb.) country; Ladino-*Medina*

neshama – (Heb.) soul

SAUDADE -- Nostalgic Longing

Rufina Bernardetti Silva Mausenbaum

Portugal is often described as having a rich and romantic past. For me, it is painful and tragic. Although I was baptized in the Catholic Church, I converted to Orthodox Judaism, the religion of my forefathers, 36 years ago and often still experience the frustration, humiliation, and shame suffered by my family (and others) for centuries. My very own origins, history, and culture have been effectively obliterated and it is, for me, a continuing and haunting loss.

But the last several years have become a particularly poignant voyage of discovery. For the first time I can talk about my family "secrets" without ridicule. The haunting soulfulness of the Portuguese *Fado* (folk music) reminds me of others like me, struggling to make sense of the secrets from a forgotten past, born out of a people who have almost disappeared, and my *Saudades* (nostalgic longing) for the past continues.

Like me, many people throughout the world are discovering their family secrets for the first time. Amongst them have been a priest in the US, who, on discovering his roots, left the priesthood after 11 years; a grandfather in New Mexico who, while dying, whispered to his grandson, "We are Jews"; and a community in Portugal that rejoined mainstream Orthodox Judaism after 500 years of isolation. It is estimated that in Brazil 34 million and in Portugal more than half the population are from *Anousim* heritage (forced converts from Judaism to Christianity).

The Jews have been a part of the Iberian peninsula for 3000 years, having arrived there with the Phoenicians, living and trading within organized communities. Judaism flourished as the only monotheistic religion before giving birth to Christianity and later to Islam. The Iberian pagans converted to Judaism readily, as did the people of North Africa. The influence of the Jewish religion, culture and language on the Mediterranean Basin was entrenched during the seven centuries of Carthaginian rule (813 to 146 BCE). Long after their defeat by the Romans, the Punic language (the West Semitic language of Carthage) continued. An interesting theory is that Hebrew might well have been the language of the Mediterranean Basin if the Romans had lost the war at Carthage!

That Portugal may have been Jewish before becoming Catholic helps explain why the first 11 printed works in Portugal were written in Hebrew, the first being the Pentateuch.

In Portugal, the oldest country in Western Europe, her borders unchanged for 800 years, there was hardly a noble or aristocratic family that was free of Jewish ("tainted") blood. Important positions—physicians, lawyers, writers, navigators and explorers in the Americas and Africa, financiers and army personnel—were occupied by *Conversos*. Much of the financing in Europe and the New World was controlled by Portuguese *Conversos*. The Spanish (and others) were known to complain that you could not do business unless you had a "Portuguese" partner ("Portuguese" being synonymous with "Jewish").

My grandmother, whose name I bear, was thought to be odd in the village where she found secrecy and anonymity because once a year (on the Day of Atonement) she used to disappear for a whole day and night. It is with pride that I remember my grandmother Rufina, who in spite of the danger to her life, managed to keep her faith. How pleased she would have been had she known her humiliation had not been in vain. That today, many years later, her granddaughter Rufina observes the *Antepura* (Yom Kippur, Day of Atonement) openly as a Jewess of Portuguese heritage.

Whenever I visit Portugal, a feeling of *deja vu* overcomes me—remnants of the past remain, of the period when Jews dominated life in Portugal. Saturday is still called Sabado (Sabbath) and Sunday (Domingo) is the first day of the week. A town outside Lisbon sells pastries packed in blue and white paper decorated with a *Magen David*. In Madeira, art and craft shops also feature this emblem. This beautiful island also knew fear and became a hiding place for many Jews. Unlike many in Portugal, the Jews of Madeira did not manage to sustain their religious identity. Today they are devout Catholics as once they were devout Jews, and the Jewish cemetery lies forgotten, neglected, and in ruin. The irony is that the Jews as a people had been in Portugal long before those who expelled and persecuted them.

On the 17th of March 1989, the president of Portugal, Mario Soares, publicly apologized to the Jewish community for the horror and cruelty of the past and linked the economic and intellectual decline of Portugal to the "expulsion" and persecution of Portugal's Jewish citizens. There had been no expulsion, only the forced conversion *en masse* of the Jews of that country. It is this important fact in history, often ignored, that is responsible for many Portuguese today being the descendants of Jews.

When looking at a map of Portugal, it is easy to see that the main centers of the Inquisition—Lisbon, Evora, and Coimbra—formed the heart of the country, the heart that destroyed its own people. Yet Portuguese

Judaism miraculously continues, especially in the community of Belmonte in northeast Portugal, where Crypto-Jews, in December 1996, rejoined mainstream Orthodox Judaism after 500 years of secrecy and fear. Living and hiding in the charming town high in the Serra da Estrela (Mountain of Stars), they managed with faith and perseverance to maintain some part of their religion all this time. As is often stated, they were Jews in all but name and Christians in nothing but form. A prayer said secretly by' Crypto-Jews on entering a church featured the words "I come here to worship neither wood nor stone, I come only to worship you, Highest Lord, who it is that governs us."

Versions of this essay appeared on the Saudades.org web site and in the Kulanu newsletter.

A Feeling of Joy

Rufina Bernardetti Silva Mausenbaum

A feeling of joy descends
slowly
Finding its resting place
within me
The images of the past now
an inspiration
Listening to the memories
fills me with tenderness
I have survived, I am here, I am alive
Connected always to my past
with love and **saudades**
For those who went before, so
I open my heart like a shrine
Unblemished by bitterness
or hate
Filled with love for them
Centuries of tender care
could not deny
Born into a perfect harmony
As humane and mature, I now
face the future
With the wholeness
of spirit that is victorious
We once more can share
The essence and purity
of life as
Jews from Sepharad.

This poem appears on the Saudades.org web site.

The Crypto-Jews

Robin Becker

This summer, reading the history of the Jews of Spain,
I learned Fra Alfonso listed "holding philosophical discussions"
as a Jewish crime. I think of the loud fights
between me and my father when he would scream that only a Jew
could love another Jew. I love the sad proud history
of expulsion and wandering, the Moorish synagogue walled
in the Venetian ghetto, persistence of study and text.
In New Mexico, the descendants of Spanish *conversos* come forth
to confess: tombstones in the yard carved with Stars of David,
no milk with meat, generations raised without pork.
What could it mean, this Hebrew script,
in grandmother's Catholic hand? Oh, New World, we drift
from eviction to eviction, go underground,
emerge in a bark on a canal, minister to kings, adapt to extreme
weather, peddle our goods and die into the future.

This poem is from *All-American Girl*, by Robin Becker, © 1996. Reprinted by permission of the University of Pittsburgh Press.

Coming to Terms

Rabbi Stuart Federow

I cannot put into words, what I just experienced. But I must try, because, as I think about it, the tears continue to run down my face, and it begins to dawn on me, through my thoughts and feelings, exactly what it must have meant to have been one of the *Anousim*, and what it might, maybe, feel like to realize that one's ancestors clearly went through hell, hiding who they were, sometimes even from family members, and feeling always alone, always afraid of discovery.

I am near the end of the process of converting a woman to Judaism. She has begun the twin tasks of researching her family and of coming to terms with her discoveries and the implications of those discoveries. Today, at lunch, we were sitting together at a favorite salad bar restaurant. I was telling her what she should expect with our Beit Din and with the Mikveh, and I made a little joke about how lucky she was not to have to go through what the men converting have to go through. Her face immediately clouded over, and she looked as though she had just been given a very difficult math problem to solve.

I asked her what was wrong, and she said, "You know, Rabbi, I just don't understand something. In the early 1970s my grandfather was dying, his heart began to fail him, blood was pooling in his hands and in his feet. And he called in a Jewish doctor to circumcise him. Why would he do that? There is no medical reason why anyone should be circumcised on his death bed, and two days later he died. Why would he want to be circumcised?"

I told her, "Possibly, because he knew he could not live like a Jew, but he wanted to die like a Jew." Her eyes immediately glazed over, as my words sank in, and then she began to sob loudly, at just one more piece of the giant mosaic that constitutes undeniable proof that her family were *Anousim*.

I read these words that I have just typed, and I cry too. At the thousands and thousands of families whose heritage remains stolen from them, at the pains their ancestors went through just to be who they were. I wish each of you could have seen the look on her face as she fully began to recognize the meaning of this discovery. What seemed obvious to me was an explosion of light to her, because she never, until that moment, put the pieces of that part of the mosaic together.

Stephen Leon, a wise rabbi in El Paso, has suggested that we designate the Ninth of Av a national day of story telling of the experience of the *Anousim* -- with great publicity, so that thousands and thousands of families may be inspired by the stories they hear to regain what remains rightfully theirs. Rabbi Leon is so right.

After the Fire

Clara Castelar

We've lain in this bed of ashes for thousands of lifetimes,
Crushed by the weight of our fear.
No ladder fell from the sky bearing
Archangels willing to be pummeled.
We didn't have the heart to pinion the cherubim
Who dared to check our attendance at autos-da-fe.
We slept beneath the rock of our regrets,
learning to dream.

Our wishes are simple now,
We want to be granted the gift of welcome,
The benison of forgiveness,
The blessing of rest after our struggle.

How shall we reclaim what was ours before the fire?
All we have left is the tiredness of centuries
Spent holding keys for doors that won't open for us.
We are weary of waiting for a bridge to cross this vacuum
An absence of mercy created around us.
How long shall we atone?
Must we make our way to God inch by inch,
Hoisting ourselves, hand over bloody hand, on the rope of your doubts?

This poem appeared in the Kulanu newsletter and occupies a special place on the
Kulanu.org web site.

In Recognition of a Martyr

Schulamith Chava Halevy

Luis de Carvajal el Mozo was the nephew, namesake and heir-designate of the first governor of Nuevo Reino de Leon. Possibly the largest land tract granted anyone by Spain, the region stretches from eastern Mexico through the US Southwest. When Luis learned from his family that he was a Jew, the impact was tremendous. A man of culture, letters and verse, who sang and played the harp, spoke several languages and possessed a grand spirit, Luis was unable or unwilling to conceal his faith. Instead, he went about trying to convince anyone he could to observe the "Law of Moses."

Carvajal was arrested, and in the cells of the Inquisition converted his cell mate, a monk, to Judaism. There he also changed his name to Joseph Lumbroso—Joseph, after the biblical dreamer, since he too had inspired dreams, and Lumbroso meaning "the Enlightened." Even after his first arrest, torture and incarceration—knowing full well that a second arrest meant the stake—he did not relent.

Joseph-Luis was denounced again by a would-be proselyte. His second arrest was characterized by religious pride and steadfastness that left its mark even on his tormentors. Luis debated those sent to convert him with eloquence, knowledge and spirit. Prayers attributed to him were recited to inquisitors a century after his death by subsequent victims. Seymour Liebman, in his seminal book, *The Jews of New Spain*, translated the words of Padre Contreras, who walked Luis to his fate: "He was always such a good Jew and he reconciled his understanding, which was very profound and sensitive, with his highly inspired Divine determination to defend the Law of God—the Mosaic—and to fight for it. I have no doubt that if he had lived before the Incarnation of our Redeemer, he would have been a heroic Hebrew and his name would have been as famous in the Bible as are the names of those who died in the defense of their law when it was necessary."

In 1996, on the 400th anniversary of his martyrdom, Casa Amistad, a group of *Anousim* in Chicago, organized events in his memory. These included a biographical play at the Newberry Library—attended at full capacity—the lighting of Hanukkah candles and the unveiling of works of art depicting the martyrdom by Chicago Latino artists. The mayor of Chicago declared the anniversary as the "Luis de Carvajal Day of Tolerance." My poem, which follows, was inspired, not only by the life of

Luis de Carvajal el Mozo, but also by the lives of *Anousim* I know, and by what Casa Amistad was able to bring about.

The word "martyr" comes from the Greek and means "to bear witness." By remembering and reminding, we extend the impact of Carvajal's heroic life and death into our time.

May his memory be blessed.

This essay and the following poem originally appeared in the Kulanu newsletter.

El Lumbroso

Schulamith Chava Halevy

That night I was so radiant
You could barely see me for my light.

Now in the incandescent dawn
I am paraded before your helpless eye.
The stakes are high
enough for me to see my angel cry.
Padre Contreras, frail and vulnerable
Murmurs why?
Listen! the flames' voice is cracking
Hear it sigh...
My flesh implodes in the fire
Together we witness it reduce to ashes
Together watch it fly.

You and I,
How we danced ever closer to the flames
--to my flesh, to its demise
Your old soul knows I could not die,
but your mind is young,
Cannot yet read the milestones of the sky.

Cloistered in my afterglow
Shawled in me
You stood in prayer
That the light I have become
Be bestowed
Upon you.

My apparition soars
Carried in your dreams.
Four hundred years in the abyss
Cannot erase
the seal
our memories
call
I can still embrace
can enter you
Breathe my eternity into your soul.

37

A Ladino Bedtime Prayer for Children

Rachel Ziona Segal

SHEMAH YISRAEL ADONAI ELOHAYNU ADONAI ECHAD
BARUCH SHEM K'VOD MALCHUTO LEM OLAM VA-ED
OYE MI HIJO CASTIGUERO DE TU PADRE Y NO DEJES LEY DE
   TU MADRE
CUATRO CANTONADAS MAY EN ESTA CASA, CUATRO
   MALCHIM QUE NOS
ACOMPANA Y NOS CUIDA DE LANTRA DE PINTA Y DE TODA
   MUERTA
SUPITANIA CON BUENO QUE NOS ACOSTEMOS, CON BUENO
   QUE NOS
LEVANTEMOS CIERRO MIS PERTAS CON SELLOS DE ABRAHAM
   AVINU Y
LLAVES DE MIRIAM MA NEVIA, QUE SANABA, MEDICINABA,
   CIENCIA,
PACIENCIA DABA A TODO HIJITO DE ISRAEL Y A MI TAMBIEN.

Hear O Israel, the Lord our God, the Lord is One.
Blessed his name whose glorious kingdom is forever.
Listen my child to the precepts of your father, and do not forget your
mother's guidance. There are four pillars in this house and four angels
who watch over us and shield us from harm and danger. May we lie down
in peace and awaken in peace. I lock my doors with Abraham's seals and
with the keys of Miriam, who was a healer and taught us patience. May
these blessings be with every child of Israel and me as well. Amen.

This prayer has been passed on for four generations in the family of Rachel Ziona Segal.

The Little Brown Box

Barbara Aiello

The little brown box contained only four items. Two buttons, one tortoise in color, the other a faded red, a wad of string and best of all, a knife. The knife held a certain fascination for me. First of all, it was so very tiny—less than two inches long, and its pearly handle contained an even tinier blade. My fat little-girl hands struggled to open it and close it, open it and close it, over and over again. The knife and its brother items slept in the brown box on a table next to my father's side of the bed. Often in early morning he let me touch them. I'd line them up, move them around and put them back into the box again.

"Why, Daddy? Why these things?" I would ask him. He would only sigh and smile his odd smile where the corners of his mouth turned down and say, "Another time, *cara*. We will talk about them another time."

Years passed. The bedroom furniture molted from second-hand to the blonde bedroom suite bought on "time" from the local furniture dealer. Different tables, but that same brown box. Daddy changed, too. Now, instead of sitting silently as my mother marched my sister and me to Catholic mass, he asked that I, his oldest, be allowed to stay home. "She should learn about my side," he said. My mother grimaced, her typical Argentine pout. But reluctantly she gave in. "Do what you want," she said, somehow resigned that one daughter of Rome was better than none at all.

So Sundays in my eighth year became a day of Jewish education for me, taught by a man well past middle age, who seemed almost frantic to share his heritage with me and the story that was to become my heritage as well.

"In Italy there were very few Jewish people," he began. "Especially in the south of Italy, where everyone was very poor and very Catholic. Your grandmother, Felicia, was the only Jewish girl in the town. As she grew older her parents were so very worried. Where would they find a Jewish boy for Felicia to marry?"

"I know what you're thinking." Daddy read my mind. "How did Nonna find Nonno? Well, I'll tell you. He came from Serrastretta, a tiny little village in the mountains. Its name means 'narrow garden,' and that's all there was there. Just skinny strips of olive trees. He hiked up the hill

39

to Nonna's town. He asked her father for her hand in marriage. But he was Catholic, not Jewish as Felicia's parents had hoped."

Daddy shook his head. "I am the first-born son. The son of a Jewish woman who, over time, had lost her connection to her Shabbat candles, her kosher home and her Havdalah light."*

I widened my eyes and jumped up. Now I got it. Daddy didn't go to mass with Mum because he was Jewish! I knew about Jewish. Jews went to church on Saturday. And they didn't have Christmas or Santa Claus. And my friend, Ellie, she went to Hebrew school to learn how to read backwards. I told all this to Daddy in one long breath. He would be proud of me that I knew so much!

Daddy laughed. "*Ragazza* (the Italian word for 'kiddo'), I guess this is enough for one Sunday," he said. I agreed. Daddy's Jewish. I dismissed this new information. So where were the funny papers?

More Sundays and more time with Daddy and his stories. It happened that I became eager for them, practically shoving my sister into her "good" coat and pushing her and Mum out the door. Then it was time for *panini*, a special grilled sandwich that Daddy made for us. I was to find out why his *panini* held only cheese. The ham was saved for the rest of us, until, following his example, I refused it as well.

"When I was about nine years old," Daddy began, "my mother told me that I was her Jewish son. I'll tell you now that I wasn't pleased. Jews were mysterious to me. To some of my friends, especially the older boys, they were hated and feared. But your Nonna, she pressed on. She revealed to me why she never ate pork or certain kinds of fish. Why she prayed in her heart and refused to bow before statues in her husband's church. She told about a special book—not shaped like a book, but rolled up. A scroll, she called it. A Torah scroll. She said the laws for living a good life were found in the Torah."

"So, Daddy, why don't you go to church on Saturdays like my friend Ellie does. Why aren't you doing Jewish things?"

"First, *cara* (the Italian word for "dear one"), the church you talk about is called a synagogue. And I don't go because...." He paused and looked down at his welder's boots. "Because I never did."

"But do you want to go now?" I hoped the answer was no. I really didn't want to give up our special Sunday mornings together.

40

"No, not now," Daddy said. "I'd rather talk to you like this. Then maybe later on, when you're grown, you'll want to go. Maybe you'll want to go in my place. You'll go for me."

Truthfully, my father knew very little about Jewish observance or tradition. He remembered only snatches of his conversations with his mother, pieces he heard nearly half a century ago, but he told them to me faithfully each Sunday morning.

Years later, when I had left home for college and then marriage, he added to his story. It was in April and now I know that it was Pesach in April of that year. My daughter Rosanna was just days old. She was his first grandchild, a wondrous event, made even more so because he was now a man in his late seventies.

"I have a gift for Rosanna," he said, pronouncing her name, "Ross-anna" in the Italian way. From his pocket he took a box and placed it on her baby tummy. Immediately I recognized it. The box with the buttons, string and knife I had seen so many years ago.

"This box is for you," he said to my baby. "The things inside were given to me by people who had lost all. People who had nothing to give. Jews gave these things to me, and I give them to you."

So finally my father told the story of the brown box. How, as a *partigiano,* an Italian resistance fighter, he had jumped into Buchenwald by parachute to light the camp for Americans and Russians who would later drop food and blankets to the Jews who had survived. As he tore open boxes and began to offer food, the Jews who received it began to repay him.

"To the first man I almost shouted. 'No! Everything has been taken from you. I cannot take from you, too.' But then I saw that this man had one thing that had not been taken. His dignity, in the face of unspeakable horror, remained. So I accepted his offer—a red button. From another, scraps of string. Then, from a small woman this button, tortoise in color. Finally, from a man too weak to stand, this very small knife. A knife he had saved, had hidden, had risked his life to keep. When he pressed the knife into my hand, I knew that taking it from him was the right thing to do."

My father continued. "It's strange, but when I accepted those things, those tiny things, a part of me accepted my Jewish roots, as well. And it seemed as though the few Jewish traditions I held so close, tiny remembrances from my mother, were now as important to me as the scraps of Jewish life I saved in the brown box."

"*Cara*," my father turned to my baby. "I was lost, but not you. For me and for my four friends at Auschwitz, may you not be lost to the Jewish people."

"Please," he said to me, "raise Rosanna as a Jew."

Three short years later my father was dead. "I will die happy if I can see Disney World," he told his Pittsburgh buddies. He was stricken as he left the park, holding Rosanna's hand. But the promise has been kept. Fulfilled in part on her first day of Hebrew school and brought to life on that day in June when Rosanna became a Bat Mitzvah.

And I learned along with her. It was difficult to put aside my fear of adopting and participating in a new tradition so late in life, and hard to stop worrying about how I looked to others who had been practicing Jews since they were children. Yet I found the courage—wrapped in string, fastened with buttons and molded with a knife—in a brown box beside my bed.

*Author's Note:
My family traces its roots all the way back to the Golden Age of Spain and the Inquisition times, when Jews were forced, under threat of torture or death for themselves and their children, to convert to Christianity. Some of my ancestors converted through force and stayed in Spain. Others fled, first to Gibraltar then to Morocco, then to Sicily, Southern Italy, and Argentina, before finally settling in America. These ancestors were "Crypto-Jews," who, like my "Nonna Felicia," practiced what little they knew about their religion in secret. But both groups, the converts and the "Crypto-Jews," fall under the "Anousim" umbrella because these Jews were forced— either to convert or to take their Jewish practices underground.

This story, © 1998 by Barbara Aiello, won second prize in the Seventh Annual Sylvia Wolens Jewish Heritage Writing Competition. It also appeared in the Kulanu newsletter.

A Converso Lament

Norman Chansky

Like so many S'fardim before us
We bent like tree branches in the wind.
And when we straightened our limbs
To assume our integrity
We were cut down by marauding crowds
In the name of God
And burned in a pyre
Or grafted onto an alien branch
Of the bough of Abraham.
We sprouted here, there, and everywhere
Though in secret.
Our offshoots were a masquerade,
A charade of our original stalk
In the name of Pi-ku-ach nefesh.
But our souls were pillaged;
Our heritage was raped;
Our faith was defaced;
Tears clung like dew drops
To every page
Of every chapter
Of our history.
Although emptied of our history,
We still kindle a candle on Shabbat eve
To recall our charred ancestors,
Betrayed by their own kinsmen
During the Inquisition,
And so that our ancestors will see
The path leading to Gan Eden.

'Though our golden links are tarnished
We extend our hands to clasp
Those of our people
As children of one family, Israel.

My 50-year Search for My Portuguese-Jewish Self

Stephen L. Gomes

Today marks the celebration of my first Rosh Hashanah as a Jew! When I entered the Mikveh at the University of Judaism in Los Angeles, it was the single defining moment of my life. It is difficult to describe in words what happened to me. It was a completion, a sense of coming full-circle, of finding and reclaiming my elusive long-lost Jewish soul, my *neshama*, for now and always — never to be lost again. All of the pain, challenges, and uncertainties I experienced over the years in this search pale by comparison with the magnificent emotional splendor of that defining moment. When Rabbi Steven Tucker of Temple Ramat Zion of Granada Hills, Rabbi Mark Diamond, and others, including my 81-year old Catholic mother and members of my Jewish community, witnessed my Return to my people, I knew I was home at last.

If I were a journalist, I could tell you my story in one sentence. On Monday, March 25, 2002, (12 Nisan 5762) before a Beit Din of three rabbis from the Los Angeles Rabbinate at the University of Judaism, Stephen Gomes, a Portuguese-American Catholic, completed his conversion to Judaism. But facts do little to convey my 50-year journey to recover the Jewish heritage of my ancestors. Nor can they communicate the challenges and uncertainties that accompanied each and every decision as I delved deeply into the mystery of self, of heritage, of Jewish identity, and of soul.

My tale could begin with the discovery in 1996 that my father's 16th century ancestor was buried in the "Field of the Jews" in the Madeira Islands off the coast of Portugal. Or it could begin with tracking relatives with my maternal great-grandmother's name, "De Quintal," who whispered on the phone in hushed tones, "You know they say we are Jews."

Instead I want to tell the story of my conversion from the highly personal perspective of self–discovery. Starting from about seven or eight years old, I began to realize that, in some important but seemingly unknowable way, I did not fit in with the rest of the kids at the Catholic schools I was sent to. By the time I was in college, the feelings began to change, becoming more insistent and impossible to ignore. I experienced a growing realization that something ineffable, undefined was calling me. But what was it? One day, in graduate school, my best friend, Stephen

Wiel, with no preamble or warning, popped a totally startling and mind-altering question to me: "Why are all your friends Jewish?" Not only did I have no answer for what I thought at the time was a completely crazy question; I couldn't begin to fathom why he asked it in the first place. But ultimately it was the first clue that put me on the track to my Return. His question stayed with me, resonated, percolated. Until one brisk Pittsburgh winter day, I woke up with the question, "Could I possibly be Jewish?"

For those of you who have been Jewish from birth, I am not sure you could put yourself in the mindset of the unsettling road of inquiry this question posed for me. It is an identity-shattering kind of question which at that time had no basis in fact. My drive to unravel the mystery of this illusive Jewish identity became like a mysterious, inexplicable compulsion.

After I received my Ph.D. I moved to Reno, Nevada. One snowy night, I found myself sitting in my hot tub with another good friend, a psychiatrist named Ed Lynn (Jewish, naturally), discussing this feeling I had. I said "Ed, is there something wrong with me?" At first he laughed about it, but then he said, "You know, that there is something called the Jewish soul or *neshama*. You might be having an experience with that phenomenon." For some reason, that really struck a chord with me.

In 1980 I moved to San Francisco. The "calling" was continuous and unrelenting. I spoke to many rabbis, and they all uniformly discouraged me. Then one day I was introduced to Rabbi David Zeller. He accepted me as a student. Unfortunately, before I could make much progress toward conversion, the rabbi's wife suddenly died and left him with three very young children to raise. He moved to Israel and my study took a detour.

For the next ten years, I filled much of my spare time studying my family history. I engaged in a lot of genealogical and historical research. It began to become increasingly evident that I could actually be a direct descendant of Jewish ancestors from the Portuguese Inquisition in 1497. I studied the history, and it convinced me to redouble my effort to convert.

I have since learned that my maternal great-grandfather might have known that he was Jewish when he entered the U.S. in Hawaii in 1868 and changed his name from Joao Baptista de Quintal to John Q.Baptist.

Right now I am trying to learn all I can about the Quintal family name and history. Recently, I had the wonderful opportunity to participate in a Portuguese Jewish Heritage Tour. While I was in Portugal, with the help of members of the Saudade-Sefarad group, I was able to locate the medieval Portuguese village of Quintal in north central Portugal; this was the source of our family name. Some of the buildings are still in use. I was amazed to find a Hebrew inscription carved into one of the solid lintel stones in one doorway's interior.

So far, I have learned that during the Portuguese Inquisition, while many Portuguese Jews fled to other countries to avoid forced conversion, most were forced to remain and convert (as opposed to Spain where most Jews fled the country). I have also learned from Inquisition archives that there were 177 cases of Judaizing (accusation that new Christians had reverted to their Jewish practices) against persons with the last name of "Gomes," and five with the surname of "de Quintal" (the name means "from the village of Quintal," which had a population of 200 men, women and children at the time).

While this history is and continues to be under-researched in Portugal, there is mounting evidence (see Netanyahu's book on the origins of the Inquisition) that this massive crime committed against the Jews of Portugal by the dominant Church and royal establishment at that time was actually motivated primarily for greed and economic confiscation. The religious accusations were primarily a diversion designed to enlist the support of the illiterate masses and incite their anger. (Remember, at that time the Church did not allow peasants to learn to read—even the Bible.)

For me, stepping into the Mikveh brought me full circle—I was home at last. The feeling is still very new and very vivid for me; I am fully certain for the first time. I truly know who I am at the core of my soul— without a trace of doubt or lingering hesitancy. This sense of certainty is a great gift.

Besides great joy, the certainty of this "knowing" also brought with it a great sadness. I felt the pain of our forefathers and ancient grandmothers, having their children, their traditions, their very heritage forcefully ripped away — seemingly forever. Somehow these events of 500 years ago became as fresh and vivid inside of me as if it happened yesterday. And now I feel a grave responsibility to rectify this loss in some way — to make it somehow worthwhile. Even if I could have only a small role in helping a few Portuguese descendants find their way back to their heritage, their true identity, their real roots, then I will be at peace.

Now I can't be in Portugal or with Portuguese and not see evidence of their Jewish heritage everywhere — in their mannerisms, superstitions, body language, words, culture, family practices, way of being in the world, their personal philosophies, customs, and stubborn propensity to debate. All of these have a root in their common Jewish ancestry.

Their continuing inability to embrace their inheritance is such a shame. But there are signs of hope that seem to be gaining some momentum — including our ground-breaking trip to Portugal. Since participating in that Portuguese Jewish reunion tour, I have spoken many times at synagogues about discovering my Portuguese-Jewish roots and what it has meant to me.

I speak about how, even in my own immediate family, these vestiges of Jewish practices persist. They are small clues into the past, but for most of us that is all we have. Just last week I discovered that my maternal great-grandfather actually had two sons named Jacob and two sons named Benjamin (of twelve sons and one daughter). I asked my mother why that would be, since I only knew about one Benjamin and one Jacob. She said it was because in her family for generations they had a peculiar tradition; as long as she could remember, they named their children after relatives who had died. So when their first son Jacob died in his first year of life, they named another son after him, and the same with Benjamin. Even my middle name, Laurence, is named after my mother's brother, who was a pilot in World War II who died trying to make sure that a German tank did not succeed in overtaking an American GI position.

Another touching remnant of our tradition is the fact that my grandmother on my father's side always baked braided Portuguese sweet bread on Friday mornings (it looked and tasted exactly like challah; the first time I saw challah I thought it was Portuguese sweet bread). As I kid I could hardly wait for Fridays because we would stop at my grandmother's house after school and have toasted fresh Portuguese sweet bread with butter and dip it in hot chocolate. My brothers and I thought it was such a delicious treat. When I asked her why she did that she said she did not know, but it made her feel good because that is what her mother and her mother's mother and all the women in her family did as far back as she could remember, from the time she was a small girl.

An early version of this article appeared in the *Journal of the Crypto-Judaic Society* <www.cryptojews.com>.

The Oak of Tears*

Ilan Braun

No time to think
Nor to lament
You must dig, right there
Deep, between the tree's roots

Quick, dig with your bare hands
The cursed bell is going to toll
& brand with shame
the coming hour
& tarnish forever your pride

Lay down, trembling, your treasure
Sacred rolls & writings of an entire life
The land which has seen you being born
Has lied to you
She is no more than a brown shroud of oblivion

And with your foot
Close up the grave of your memory
Now they can come & seize you
& put you in chains

At the far end of your garden
At the old oak's bottom
Lies, for ever,
Your soul

---

* This poem is based on the true story of a Spanish Jew who, before being expelled from
Spain, buried his writings and Torah scrolls.

High Holy Days Among Spanish Marranos (Anousim)

Gloria Mound

Five centuries ago, the Days of Awe among the Spanish Marranos were indeed regarded as such by them, but uppermost was FEAR, of being discovered by the Inquisition.

Therefore, the fact that Rosh Hashanah is but 10 days from Yom Kippur made most secret communities weigh which of the two festivals was paramount. To take time off from work twice in such close succession, whatever excuse they wished to make, or if self-employed, to be seen desisting from work first for two consecutive days and then another day but 10 days later, was for the majority just too risky.

And so in the passage of very few years after the expulsion of the Jews from Spain, and particularly in the Balearic Isles, only Yom Kippur was observed. The Marranos, or *Chuetas*, as they were called on the Island of Majorca, called Yom Kippur "*El Dia Puro.*" Fasting was something that they found the easiest to do without detection. It was to make a gathering for prayers that was far more difficult. Yet somehow they managed it throughout the centuries. The fact that our calendar is lunar was a tremendous help to isolated groups.

One of the most thrilling reports of Marranos praying together in secret was reported in the 1930s, when Ezriel Carlebach, editor of the *Jewish Daily Forward* in New York, found himself in the capital of the Balearic Isles, Palma-de-Majorca, on Kol Nidre night. The biggest problem for the American was to convince the *Chuetas* that he was indeed a Jew, and wished to pray with them. After so many centuries the *Chuetas* knew almost no Hebrew, but the one common word between them and Carlebach was *Adonai*. Later, when this had convinced them, Carlebach saw how the prayers, even in Spanish, still had the form and order of the service that so many Jews around the world know.

We are told that the original Kol Nidre prayer was composed by those suffering the tortures of the Inquisition.

In my visits and studies to the more tolerant, smaller Balearic Isles, especially Ibiza and Formentera, the third and fourth largest ones, the more jovial Festival of Succoth, with its pastoral, agricultural emphasis, seems to have been far easier to observe.

To this day, the village of San Miguel has a Fiesta which is set by the moon's cycle and usually seems to fall on the intermediate days of

Succoth. There is a procession around the village, with a proportion of the men dressed in creamy white shawls fringed at the corners. In their arms they carry an exact replica of the *lulav*, but the *etrog* is missing. Another nearby place has a 16th century folk song of how the Jews, Moors, and Christians celebrated Fiestas together at the time when, officially, no practicing Jew was allowed to live in Spain!

Here in Israel we are free to observe our festivals, but if our forefathers in times of danger had not somehow remembered and tried to practice, would there still be Jews and a State of Israel? I admit I stand in Awe of their tenacity and faith, and I try to remember them in my own prayers.

The Sephardic Experience In the Holocaust

Yitzchak Kerem

The heart of the Judeo-Spanish-speaking Sephardic world, the Jewish communities of Yugoslavia and Greece, were overwhelmingly annihilated in the Holocaust by the Nazis and their Axis counterparts. Very few Sephardic Jews from these countries returned to their homes after World War II. Sephardic communities in Rumania and Vienna were also destroyed in the Holocaust. The Jews of Bulgaria were spared due to public protest and parliamentary opposition, and sent to forced labor, but the Sephardic Jewish communities in the areas annexed by the Bulgarians (Greek Thrace and Yugoslavian Macedonia) were deported by the Bulgarian army to the Nazi death camps or murdered by the Bulgarians on the Danube River.

In neutral Turkey, the Sephardic communities remained intact, but they had to contend with the Varlik Vergisi luxury tax which Turkey placed on minorities in order to appear tough on Jews and other unwanted groups—in anticipation of German attack and occupation. Many Jews could not pay and were sent to forced labor in Askale and other camps. Despite this, Turkey did exhibit altruism in allowing Jewish refugees fleeing Nazism in northern Europe and southern Greece to pass through its territory to Eretz-Israel (Palestine).

* * *

Yugoslavia. In April 1941, Germany conquered Yugoslavia, and the country was divided among its allies. Some 15,000 of the 82,000 pre-war Yugoslavian Jews (30,000 of whom were Sephardi) survived the war. Some 2,000 had survived in camps in Italy, and some 2-3,000 Jews had joined the partisans. Throughout Yugoslavia, most of the Jews were interned in camps by the end of 1941 and liquidated by the middle of 1942. Others escaped to the partisans or found refuge in Albania and were protected by Muslims.

In Croatia, the Italians established internment camps to protect the Jews from the Germans and the Croatian Ustashe, but the Croatians established death camps in order to exterminate the Jews in accordance with the German preference and Final Solution. The Ustashe established death camps on the Island of Pag in the Dalmatia region, and the infamous death factory Jasenovac. The Croatians totally destroyed both the Ashkenazic Central synagogue and the new glorious Sephardic synagogue of Sarajevo.

In Bosnia, more than 10,000 of the region's 12,000 Jews died in the Holocaust. Like the Jews of Croatia, Bosnian Jews were rounded up beginning in the summer of 1941 and continued intermittently thereafter. By August 1942 the Jews of Sarajevo had disappeared. Since the late 1930s, there had been an atmosphere of anti-Semitism in this mostly-Muslim city. Nazi propaganda and anti-Jewish hostility, based on the 1936-1939 riots in Eretz-Israel and stirred up by the Jerusalem Mufti Haj Amin al-Husseini, incited the local Muslim population.

Bulgaria. In Yugoslavian Macedonia under Bulgarian military occupation, conditions for the Jews were harsh and much anti-Jewish legislation was promulgated. According to the Dannecker-Belev agreement of February 1943, Bulgaria was to deport 20,000 Jews, 12,000 from Yugoslavian Macedonia and Greek Thrace in the new occupied areas and 8,000 Jews from "Old Bulgaria" (from the Jewish communities of Plovdiv and Kustendil). Only the Jews from the new occupied areas in Yugoslavia and Greece were deported to Treblinka. Bulgarian and German soldiers sent Jews from Cavalla and Cuomotini, Greece, on the Karageorge boat, which departed from Lom, and somewhere on the shores of the Danube River executed all of them; the boat never arrived in Vienna to meet the train to Treblinka.

Plans to deport the Jews of Kustendil, Plovdiv, and other cities in Old Bulgaria were cancelled. This was due to protest in the Subranie (the Bulgarian Parliament) by the Righteous Gentile Dimitir Peshev, the deputy-speaker who also represented Kustendil; Bishop Kiril of Plovdiv, who complained to the King and threatened to organize civil disobedience; Metropolitan Stefan of Sofia, other appeals by unions, writers, and personalities; bribes by Kustendil Jews to regional Bulgarian officials and the local KEV (Commissariat for Jewish Affairs); and many contacts by Bulgarian Jews with influential Bulgarian gentiles.

Greece. Greek Jewry, which was overwhelmingly Sephardic, but consisted of Judeo-Greek Romaniote communities in Ioanina and Chalkis, mixed Sephardic-Romaniote communities in Thessaly and Athens, and separate Judeo-Italian and Romaniote communities in Corfu, lost 89 percent of its Jews in the Holocaust; some 67,000 perished out of 77,000 Jews, including 1,700 Sephardic Jews from Rhodes who were under the Italian Protectorate until autumn 1943.

The Salonikan Jewish community, which was the most prolific Sephardic cultural and religious center in the world and which dominated the city as a plurality or majority throughout most of the 450 years since the Spanish expulsion, suffered greatly in the Holocaust; its pre-World War II population of 56,000 was almost totally annihilated. Ninety-eight percent of its Jewish community, 54,000 Sephardic Jews, died after deportation to Auschwitz-Birkenau, Treblinka, or in Greece. Only Polish Jewry was exterminated in a larger percentage (99 percent). The Salonikan Jewish population was so large that the deportations took several months.

In Athens, Rabbi Eli Barzilai was requested by the new German commander Stroop, who had succeeded in destroying the Warsaw Ghetto and deporting most of its half-million Jews, to hand over lists of the members of the Jewish community. He was given an extension of 48 hours to prepare a new communal list and utilized the extension to burn existing lists and discreetly notify members of the Jewish community amassed in the synagogue for a meeting. Barzilai signaled the Jews to do what they thought was right, resist German orders, and flee; Barzilai agreed to flee to the mountains with his family under the protection of ELAS, the military wing of the Greek leftist resistance movement. While some 800 Jews reported to the Nazis weekly at the synagogue, most Jews were influenced by Barzilai and either went into hiding in the large Athens area or started fleeing from Greece via the illegal immigration network to Eretz-Israel. This network transported Greek Jews by small fishing boats from the eastern coast of the Evia Peninsula to Cesme, Turkey, and then on to Eretz-Israel. The Jews were put up in inns or refugee camps in Izmir, and then sent by train to Aleppo for two weeks of interrogation by the British intelligence. Some 3000 Jews were saved through the operation, which was jointly coordinated by the Mossad Lealiyah Bet of Eretz-Israel and the ELAS-EAM movement.

The arrest of the Jews of Athens occurred on Friday and Saturday, March 24-25, 1944, when the Jews came to register and expected to be given matzot for Passover. Instead some 800 were arrested and taken to the Haidari concentration camp for 7-8 days before being deported to Birkenau. The Turkish nationals were released and eventually sent to Turkey by train. Swiss subjects were also released.

In Thessaly, most of the more than 2000 Jews survived since they went to the resistance in the mountains near their cities of Larisa, Volos, Trikala, and Karditza. Their rabbis had the insight and courage to advise their community members to flee.

Salonikan and other Greek Jews, numbering some 15,000, most of whom had migrated to Paris, Lyons, and Marseilles in the 1930s, were targeted specially by the Nazis for deportation. In Paris, 1060 Greek Jews were arrested and sent several days later to Auschwitz.

Salonikan Jewry was the major workforce in Auschwitz-Birkenau in 1943-44. Jacko Maestro, a 14-year-old Solikan boy, coordinated the daily work schedule in Auschwitz for 16,000 inmates and saved many Jews through his efforts. Similarly boxer Jacko Razon smuggled 25-liter soup barrels daily from the Buna kitchen. Salonikan men and women comprised a fourth of the medical experiment victims in Auschwitz. Over 1000 Salonikan Jews were sent to the destroyed Warsaw ghetto to set up a labor camp of Auschwitz, and some of them participated in the two Polish Resistance revolts there in August and October 1944. Greek Jews began the Sonderkommando revolt in Birkenau on 7 October 1944 in crematoria 3 and 4, and Yitzchak Baruch placed the bomb which blew up creamatorium #3.

Turkey. In 1933, with the rise of the Nazis to power in Germany, Turkey admitted some 300 leading Jewish-German scholars, doctors, lawyers, artists, and musicians. The arrival of these eminent refugees incurred the wrath of the German community of Istanbul, which had courted and supported the activities of Nazi diplomats, merchants, and spies to undermine Turkey's support of its Jews. The German community allied with Christian nationalist groups who also sought to expel the Jews. The Nazis also attempted to plant anti-Semitism within Turkish society, which resulted in the 1934 riots against the Jews in Turkish Eastern Thrace.

Pressured by both Germany and England, neutral Turkey was torn between the two and did not desire to antagonize either. Germany requested in 1942 return of Jewish refugees who fled from her occupation and sought refuge in Turkey. Britain pressured Turkey not to let in Jewish refugees so as not to create pressure for their migration to Eretz-Israel (Palestine). This was to appease the Arabs in their opposition to Jewish migration and fear that this would contribute to the eventual establishment of a Jewish State.

By December 1942, the Jewish Agency set up a united Rescue Committee (*Vaad Hatsala*) of the Jewish Yishuv of Eretz-Israel with offices in Geneva and Istanbul since both were in neutral countries that bordered countries that were under German rule. Turkey was also a transfer point for refugees to be sent to Eretz-Israel. After the Struma boat tragedy, Turkey was extremely cooperative in allowing Jewish Holocaust refugees to stay in transit and pass through. Even though the British cabinet officially decided in July 1942 that any Jew who succeeded in escaping from occupied German control and reaching the shores of Turkey would be issued a visa to Palestine and sent by the British authorities to Palestine, British Foreign Secretary Lord Cranborne only announced this to the Turkish officials in August 1943.

In France, the historian Stanford Shaw estimated that as many as 10,000 Turkish Jews were saved by the Turkish diplomats due to their neutral status; they were sent back to Turkey by train.

In Turkey, the Varlik Vergisi, the luxury tax, was a major factor motivating most of Turkish Jewry to eventually leave the country. Approved in the Turkish Parliament in November 1942, failure to pay made the defaulter's property liable to seizure and sale. And the defaulter himself was deported to a labor camp in eastern Anatolia. Eight hundred Jews were sent to the Askale camp, where 15 of them died.

Rumania. Little has been written about the annihilation of the Sephardim in Rumania in the Holocaust. In 1940, there were 10-12,000 Sephardim in that country. The majority of these Jews were annihilated in the Holocaust, either in local concentration camps, through transfer to Transnistria and being killed in that region, or deportation to Auschwitz. On 21 January 1941, during the Fascist Legionnaire Rebellion, the Ca'al Grande (Large Synagogue) of Bucharest was burned down and the Ca'al Cicu (the Small Synagogue, also called *Ca'al Cadosh Shalom*) was used for services. With the Soviet invasion on 23 August 1944, the communities renewed their activities. Most who remained moved to Israel in the mass immigration of Rumanian Jewry in 1949. Rumanian dictator Ceaucescu closed down the Ca'al Cicu.

*   *   *

Most of these details of the Sephardic experience in the Holocaust are unknown in the Jewish world. Whether due to ignorance or prejudice, the Sephardim have been continually excluded from Holocaust historiography, education, museum exhibitions, and reparations. While there has been some rectification since the 1980s, the general public and the Jewish world still do not know that non-Ashkenazi Jews were part of the Holocaust experience and the Nazi design.

La Yave de Espanya*

Music and Lyrics (Ladino and English) by Flory Jagoda

Onde sta la yave ke stava in kashon?
Mis nonus la trusheron kon grande dolor
De su kaza de Espanya, de Espanya,
S'huenyos de Espanya

Where is the key that was in the drawer?
My forefathers brought it with great pain
From their house in Spain,

Dreams of Spain

Onde sta la yave ke stava in kashon?	Where is the key that was in the drawer?
Mis nonus la trusheron kon grande amor	My forefathers brought it with great love
Disheron a laz fijos, esto es il korason	They told their sons, this is the heart
De muestra kaza de Espanya, de Espanya	Of our home in Spain,
S'huenyos de Espanya	Dreams of Spain
Onde sta la yave ke stava in kashon	Where is the key that was in the drawer?
Mis nonus la trusheron kon grande amor	My forefathers brought it with great love
La dyeron a los nyetos a meter la a kashon	They gave it to their grandsons
Muestra yave de Espanya, de Espanya,	For them to keep it in the drawer
S'huenyos de Espanya	Our key from Spain, Dreams of Spain

*Composer's note:

When the Jews were expelled from Spain in the 15th century, legend has it that each family took with it the key to their home, treasuring it and passing it on through the centuries from father to son. Indeed, whenever a person was given a gift of great value or importance he was admonished to care for it like *la yave in kashon* (the key in the drawer). This legend was very much alive in my childhood and to this day I have an old key on my wall, a little bit like those long ago Jews, in nostalgia for what was lost in my own exile.

This song is taken from *The Flory Jagoda Songbook: Memories of Sarajevo*, © 1993 by Tara Publications.

Candles of Faith

Music by Dahlia Blech
Lyrics by Rosalie Sogolow

From mother to child,
Father to son,
All reconciled
To tell stories of old,
Rich traditions to hold.

One people by day,
Children of Spain
Longing to stay;
Lit, deep in the night
Candles of faith.

Years passed, dreams were filled with promise;
Merchants and scholars
Flourished through the centuries.
Wise men prayed and studied Torah,
Children played as proud Senoras
Taught the social graces,
Ran the home
and kindled Sabbath lights—
          Candles of faith.

Forced from their land,
Cast out and made to wander;
Jews of Spain had to change their faith or die.
But some Marranos vowed to remain
And live their secret lives….

From mother to child,
Father to son,
All reconciled
To tell stories of old,
Rich traditions to hold.

One people by day,
Children of Spain
Longing to stay;
Lit, hidden from sight,
Candles of faith.
Burning through the night….
Candles of faith.

Ashkenazim

*The Yiddish-speaking Jews of Eastern European heritage,
including those originating in Germany, Russia,
Poland, and Scandinavia*

Avremel the Tailor

Herman Taube

Everybody in Konstantin
knew Avremel the tailor,
"Die Sheyne Sarah," his wife,
and Friedele and Rochelle,
his twin daughters.
Their home was quite old
but well kept and clean.
Sarah was as goodhearted
as she was beautiful,
she worked from day break
until late at night, cleaning,
helping her husband, cooking
and serving free meals
to poor yeshiva students.
In her believing heart
there was one hope and prayer:
God would fulfill her goal,
Avremel and she would live
to see Friedele and Rochelle
under the canopy…
One day the whole family
was snatched away by the Nazis.
They were stacked in box cars
with all Konstantin Jews
and shipped off to Birkenau.
They ate mouldy bread and soup
made from weeds.
First Sarah got dysentery
and was taken "to the clinic."

Friedele and Rochelle
were selected for experiments
in the twin observation center
of Obersturmfuhrer Dr. Mengele.
Avremel worked in a
"commando"
sewing burlap bags for clothes
being shipped to the Reich.
One day he recognized a dress
he himself had made for his
Sarah.
He stopped working for a
moment
wiping his tears from his face.
The SS sentry-whip came down
on his shaved head. Avremel
collapsed, blood running down
his face.
"This is my Sarah's dress!" he
mumbled.
A kapo began swinging with his
rubber stick at Avremel's face.
He fell to the ground and died
holding Sarah's dress in his
arms…
The other inmates were jealous:
"Er iz geshtorben wie a
Mentsch!"
He died like a real Mentsch!

This poem originally appeared in *Between the Shadows* by Herman Taube (Dryad Press 1986).

A Survivor's Husband (To Susi)

Herman Taube

Often at night,
I hear you sigh,
it sounds like weeping,
groaning. You shriek
out brief sentences:
Riga, Kaiserwald,
a ship named "Bremenhaffen,"
a camp named "Stutthof."
You yammer about a raging
war, cities crumbling,
mothers raped, smothered babies,
men and women driven
into the Baltic Ocean...
I wake up when you scream,
look at your beautiful face,
listening to your heavy breathing,
I curse and hate your dreams
who torture you
for decades now.
Morning after
you dress in style,
your eyes glow,
laughing, hurrying to work,
you deal gently
with your customers,
charm them with your smile.
But I carry all day
your fears and grief.
Your memories, like heavy
rocks pull me downward,
torment my soul,
patiently I bear the load
of your pain,
I pray every day
for peaceful nights;
for the past
to pass away!...

This poem appeared in *Between the Shadows* by Herman Taube (Dryad Press 1986).

What I Learned from Living Through the Holocaust

Max Amichai Heppner

The Holocaust engulfed the first 11 years of my life. I was born in 1933, the year Hitler took power in Germany. I lived in the Netherlands, which became home to many Jewish Germans who fled across the border. As soon as I was able to understand adult conversations, I constantly heard about the dangers faced by my Jewish relatives.

After the Nazis took over my homeland as well, I felt their impact personally. On the run for over two years, I hid with a farm family in a remote area in the south of the Netherlands.

Afterwards, I talked of this period mainly as an incomprehensible catastrophe. Now I want to refocus and see the experience instead as something I can learn from. Here are some of the things I see with newly opened eyes.

Love. I would not have survived had my foster family not given me a home and a hiding place. My foster mother took me into her heart with unconditional love. She wasn't particularly demonstrative (which is what I had equated with mother love), but she was all-accepting. She treated me as kindly as she treated her own children.

I also wouldn't have survived if other people around me hadn't acted selflessly as well. In my case "it took a village" to save a child.

The value of money. The war beggared my family. After my mother and I, the only survivors in our family, came back to our hometown of Amsterdam, we had only debts and no assets. Most of our possessions, furniture, household items, and toys had been stolen.

Once we moved to the United States, I remember lacking two cents to go to a movie at lunch time with my friends in high school. Yet over the years, we regained a reasonable level of prosperity. In the process, I learned that money is merely a medium of exchange. There is as much around as you need when you let go of giving it so much importance. It's a person's view of money that measures him or her, not the amount he or she has piled up.

The value of life. I came out of the Holocaust feeling utterly victimized. Living out the victim role for many years showed me that there is no merit in that game. It can get you attention and rewards, but there is no joy in receiving them. Now I'm happy just being me. I have gained the inner confidence that my soul is pure, my heart is loving, and my presence is enjoyable to many around me without me having to put on an act.

Forgiveness. After the war, I had a dream in which I saw all inhabitants of Germany drown in the ocean. I felt that they roundly deserved this, and when it didn't happen in reality, I consigned them to Hell in my heart.

I was constantly judging. I saw Jewish people as wholly righteous and the rest of the world as more or less willing participants in the Holocaust. Now I see that judgment blinds me to beauty. I have stopped blaming "whoever" for the Holocaust, and I have replaced hate with gratitude just for being alive. I have come to believe there must be a grander meaning and purpose to life than is immediately apparent.

Equality. I was born into a family of wealth and status. If it wasn't for the Holocaust, I could have lived a life of ease and comfort. Especially as a youth, I was mad as hell for having been deprived of this lifestyle.

A look at where this was taking me showed me that as a rich kid I might have missed the chance to see all people as equal before God. I now know that having money (or even the things that money can buy, like a good education) doesn't make me a better person. Nor does lacking it make me a worse one.

I have met many Holocaust survivors whose distinguishing trait is their dignity. People who once were forced to wear prison uniforms, do degrading work, and suffer unspeakable insults, assaults, and indignities now wear attractive and appropriate clothes, do meaningful work, and treat people around them with respect. I learned that dignity is inside a person, not in their externalities.

Authority. I was born into a society that idolized authority. Through my experiences, I learned that even authority of the most autocratic type must be resisted even if the potential penalties are great. No matter what insignia of power some superior wears on his epaulets, I (as an "inferior") cannot escape responsibility for my actions by claiming I was just following orders.

Conclusion. Now that I am 69 and review my life, I am glad at having released anger, resentment, and judgment. However, I still want to say to the Universe, "Couldn't you perhaps have found a less painful way to teach me lessons?" No voice has come from Heaven to answer. All I know is that I don't have a prospectus of alternative curricula. I don't know whether I could have achieved the happiness and contentment I now enjoy by some other path. There was no other path, and so I appreciate the walk I walked.

Kaddish De Rabbanan

Marjorie Stamm Rosenfeld

Grandfather Graybeard
ate a three-minute egg each morning.
Looking like a guest just come in
with his hat on,
he blessed breakfast;
he blessed the bread,
he blessed the egg,
and the giver of eggs—God.
Something always eluded him.
On its way in
the egg dripped and caught,
shone viscous and yellow in the bristles of his beard,
a bauble for children;
while framed,
the rabbis of every principal city in Russia—
the Rabbi of Minsk and the Rabbi of Pinsk, for instance—
sat on the wall like handwriting.

Grandfather walked down the hall
in his white underwear (with his head well covered)
or wore black broadcloth.
Sometimes he performed the penny-bestowing ceremony.
This was private and confidential.
Produced mysteriously from his pocket,
the gift of dull, thumbed copper
gleamed, winked at us from between fat fingers,
left off being common coin,
became a thing of value.

My grandfather was a rabbi at sixteen,
who had read Spinoza and discovered what was the matter with
    his mind,
who had written a book on Genesis,
who every Friday afternoon spent two hours in the bathroom
    tearing paper for the whole family
        so that the work of hands
            might not sully the Sabbath.

In the evening
we stayed on the porch late,
watching the stars light up one by one
till it was finally night.
And we heard the breath of the house behind us,
hushed and waiting,
saw how, when he went in,
it closed around him.

They are all gone:
the shtetls of Minsk and Pinsk, the Vilna yeshiva,
even Chelm with its fools.
There is no place now for old Jews.
Grandfather, my childhood lives
in that fragile, broken shell in front of you.

This poem originally appeared in *Southwest Review*. The poet attests that everything in the poem is true except, perhaps, the unlikely detail about her grandfather's age at ordination.

Almost Rushin' To (Almost) Learn Russian

Sue Tourkin-Komet

My four grandparents, may they rest in peace, would be turning over in their graves, and probably with a bit of *Simcha* in their hearts. They, all four, were Russian Jews who crossed the Atlantic Ocean and the Chesapeake Bay to Baltimore, Maryland—and through the Gulf of Mexico, up the Mississippi River, eventually to Milwaukee, Wisconsin, to save their lives (and ours, eventually) from pogroms, the Czars, Communism, poverty, and, later, Hitler.

They all, all four, and many more like them, were Russian Jewish Yiddish speakers in the US, and all their children—my parents, aunts, and uncles—became Perfect English (or American, if you insist) speakers, with perfect grammar, perfect spelling, colons, semi-colons, and the like. (My Dad was a High Speed English telegraphic operator in World War II for the U.S. Army Air Corps overseas, and there was no room for error.)

Three out of my four grandparents died before my entry on earth, so I heard neither their perfect Yiddish nor their passable English. When I was 5, my one living Grandma (we didn't even know the words *Bubbie* and *Zaidie*) had taught me two tiny phrases in Russian, and for some queer reason, I loved them and remembered them forever. Now, a century after their migration to the US, and 34 years after my immigration to our Land of Israel, they'd be shocked, amazed, pleased or displeased to know that I, their hyphenated American-Israeli, young-looking yet middle-aged granddaughter is now literate in Russian—semi-fluent, albeit with my strong, give-away *Amerikanski aksent*.

The best 900 shekels I've spent on myself in a long time was the tuition I paid in 2001 to the Peoples' University, a.k.a. Beit Ha'am, in our downtown Jerusalem for my first full year of Beginners' Russian—meeting only once a week, but for an intensive 90-minute session, starting and ending promptly, no classroom breaks, no goofing around, and no discipline problems.

Surely not the same as the intensive Six Days a Week Academic Ulpan for Hebrew that I took at the Hebrew University my first year here, the year after the Six Day War, at the tender age of 19. I was on an advanced level of Hebrew already, on my first day here, and I had known the Hebrew alphabet from young childhood in the US at Hebrew School. Plus I heard Hebrew in synagogue, 52 weeks a year, albeit in prayers, psalms, songs, and "reading in unison."   I had no Advanced Headstart introduction in Russian to aid my uncomfortable "comfort level."   I was eager to learn, but scared to death of it. Now it was my Middle Aged Brain that needed to learn and memorize, starting off with that fearsome-looking Russian alphabet.

From the word "go," we students at Beit Ha'am all fell in love with our teacher, Sofi. She started it all by loving us all—even before she'd met us. And we were a challenge! She is the epitome of what Russian Jews have to offer us here—100% Jewish, Zionist, religious, academic, very intelligent, serious, humorous, diligent, orderly, optimistic, respectful, dedicated, and flexible enough to adjust a lesson plan on the spot every time that someone—usually me—asked a relevant and provocative question about a word, spelling, meaning, confusion, or pronunciation. Sofi was prepared for the best and she was prepared for the worst.

She took a real mixed bag of students, and those six of us who made it through the year—with one snowstorm, many rainstorms, many Arab terrorists' bullets and mortar shells "raining down" on my Gilo neighborhood as well as my neighborhood bus being attacked by a suicide/homicide terrorist bomber, countless suicide bombings all over Jerusalem and all over Israel—we survivors came out of it fluent in our reading and writing (certainly not reading Dostoevski or Chekhov or the likes of them), knowing past, present, and future tenses, simple conversation and greetings, and a basic vocabulary which has stimulated most of us to want to learn more and to grow with it.

I always practiced my weekly lessons with Gilo bus riders who are Russian speakers, after politely asking them for their permission, or, by going to "my" pool or "my" public library to talk with the European-mannered, proudly Jewish, retired former engineers, now guards, who were honored and delighted to help me out, despite my atrocious *Amerikanski aksent*. Being able to laugh at myself lightened things up.

My only dilemma now, as more and more Russian speakers on the buses have cell-phones, and the quieter ones read their newspapers in Russian, is: To be or not to be? To be the American that I am, and **not** eavesdrop and not glance at their newspapers? Or, to be the Israeli that I am, and eavesdrop on their Russian and/or stick my nose inside of their Russian newspapers to excite my curiosity as to what I really understand?

Using my Middle Aged Brain to remember everything I learned is challenging! When I spoke some semi-fluent, small-talk Russian in the Shuk, in front of my regular and veteran Sefaradi greengrocers, they laughed and asked me if I was aiming to find myself a Russian-speaking *chattan* (bridegroom)—and I didn't even know how to respond to their Israeli *chutzpadiche* question!

When in synagogue each Sabbath, I sometimes follow the prayers in Russian and not in my English, for sure, and not only in the normative Hebrew either. What would my *babushkas* and *dedushkas*, grandmas and grandpas, say to that?

Thank you, Sofi, for helping me get a little closer to my Russian roots, of which I am proud. I am honored to consider myself a cousin of these idealistic, top-notch Russian Jews—even though I shall never ever really be able to speak with them in their *mammaloshen*, certainly not quickly or on a deep literary level. *Bolshei spacibah*—a big thanks, Sofi. *Dosvedanyah*—until we *rendez-vous*.

Which reminds me. Thank Heavens I suffered through six years of French studies in the US, because the rudiments of French helped form the Russian language, and Russian vocabulary is packed with derivations of French (and Latin) words. *Merci beaucoup* to my past French teacher— she was a Russian-American Jewish woman, but I never figured out if she knew Russian.

This article appeared in *Horizons: The Jewish Family Journal* and was originally published by the Hagshama Department of the WZO <www.wzo.org.il>.

Mizrahim

Jews originally from the Middle East and North Africa

I'm One of 'Them' Too

Eva R. Yelloz

I was seven and considered myself a "mature" second grader, yet I never encountered a Jew who wasn't of Ashkenazi descent like myself. Then I met Jacqueline. She had huge amber eyes and thick mahogany curls. Her lashes were like silky fringes, the lower ones touching her cheek. Unlike most of us, she had only one Hebrew name. It wasn't the generic *Sara Leah* or *Chava Rivka*; her name was *Yaffa*— "beauty."

My classmates and I were English speakers and in our second year of learning *Ivrit* (Hebrew). We attended an all girls' Hebrew day school in the Bronx, New York. Like more than half of the girls in my class, I was the child of immigrants, European-born myself. But Jacqueline was different—her accent seemed throaty for a young girl. She behaved more maturely than we did and exuded a unique aura. She wore skirts with thin pleats and blouses trimmed in crocheted lace.

The girls in my class were not too kind to strangers. We stared at her while she struggled to read English aloud. We even snickered at her guttural Hebrew reading of the *Modeh Ani* in our morning prayers. Looking back at those innocent years, I realize how cruel we were. Today, my ear's recollection tells me that her Hebrew pronunciation was perfect.

One unforgettable evening, while trimming green beans with my mother, she asked, "Nu, how's school?" I quickly answered, "There's a new girl in my class." Facing my mother, I said, "Some of the girls say she's a *Frenk Parech*." Like an unexpected flash of summer lightning, my mother raised her hand and slapped my cheek. "Never say that again! We're all Jews, no matter where we come from." Her blue-green eyes were ablaze with anger.

I held my wet hand over my hot face as stinging, salty tears began to flow. I could not speak. I dared not ask what I said wrong. Then my mother explained the derogatory term I had just used. "A *Frenk Parech* is **not** a nice way to describe a Jew who comes from a French-speaking country." I asked, "Why? Isn't it something like "Frenchie?"

My Warsaw-born mother explained. *Frenk* meant French and *Parech* meant pockmarked. She continued, telling me that facial scars resulting from a skin condition caused by a bacteria-borne illness transmitted though water were common in people from North African and Middle Eastern countries. She went on to say that European Jews used this expression to describe their brethren from those lands. She made me promise to NEVER repeat that reference. I nodded my head "yes." The subject was closed. The next morning at school I decided to become friends with the beautiful girl with the French accent.

I don't remember when Jacqueline left my school or under what circumstances. But one September, she did not return. No one seemed to notice but me.

Years went by before I'd meet another non-Ashkenazi person. During those years, I learned from my mother's uncle that our Polish family had Turkish roots. The fascination and inclusion into Sephardic culture did not end there. I married a man whose mother was born in Izmir and whose father was a third generation Tiveriani—born in Tiberias, Israel. I did not plan this—it just happened. I have since immersed myself in the buried treasure of a past filled with old gold and colorful jewels.

During one of my many holiday cooking ventures, I invited a couple for the *Purim Seuda*. My house resonated with the sound of CDs of Mediterranean-influenced Israeli music. I also played my favorite tapes of *Mizrahi hazanut*. I sang along with the singers in Ladino, Judeo-Arabic, and Hebrew. The dining room atmosphere was hopping, as I could not help but dance while I fed my guests. For dessert I served baklava along with *Hamantaschen* while my husband prepared his own special blend of jasmine tea, scented with freshly picked *na'na* (mint leaves) from our garden.

That evening, the phone rang several times. Each caller was announced to us by one of our kids. One call came from my Syrian girlfriend in New York – a Shweky. Another call was from "Mama" Ruthy ('Mama' being the Iraqi term for grandma), and finally one from our Kurdish neighbor, Tito. My husband and I spoke briefly to each caller. We wished them a happy holiday and explained that we had company.

After the last call, one of our guests looked at me curiously. She said, "I've always wanted to ask you—how come all your friends have strange sounding names? They are so different, not like ours."

My lips curled into a smile. I could not enlighten her as my mother, z"l, did to me so many years ago. "Do their names disturb you?" I asked. Flustered, she shook her head back and forth with a comical motion, like a metronome keeping time. "It's just funny, an Ashkenaz couple like you two with all these unusually named friends," she retorted.

It was time to gently burst her bubble. I said, "Didn't you know that my husband is a Sephardi *Tahor*—a pure Sephardi—from both sides?"

Her royal blue outlined eyes widened with surprise. Incredulously, she said, "No, I can't believe it! You must be joking. But he's so light and looks so European."

I realized she was of a different generation—raised in another time zone. She is Israeli of Lithuanian descent whose family emigrated to Israel in the early 1920s. In those days, Ashkenazim and Sepharadim kept to themselves and 'intermarriage' was shunned and not too common. Only a few decades later, the State of Israel was established and all cultures intermingled – although not painlessly.

My friend showed her true colors that evening. I handled her insensitive remarks with humor. "You know what?" I grinned. "I'm one of THEM, too."

At that moment, my husband began to pour a cup of his special aromatic tea for each of us. Everyone "aaahed" at the lovely fragrance in the air. Jasmine bouquet with a touch of Moroccan spearmint—two enchanting ingredients from two different worlds. So delightful, *n'est-ce pas*?

American, Iraqi, Jewish— So It Makes Sense for Me To Live in Israel

Loolwa Khazzoom

My identity is tied to several different worlds: I grew up in the United States, but for me, America is largely a place of life experience and nostalgia—my home, but not the place that reflects my core identity. I do not see myself in American imagery, holidays, rituals or history. I guess it comes down to the fact that my primary identity is that of a Jew, and that for me, being a Jew is inextricably intertwined not only with Israel, but with Iraq. That's where my father came from before fleeing in 1950 to Israel, where he became a citizen. In 1958, he settled in the United States. As his daughter, I am an Israeli citizen.

My connection with Iraq is more complicated. I have never been there, but I sing and pray in the Iraqi dialect of Judeo-Arabic, the language of Jews indigenous to the region. I follow the Iraqi traditions for all Jewish holidays. I have an Iraqi accent when I pray in Hebrew, although I have purposely unlearned sounding Iraqi when I speak, partly because nobody here could understand me, and partly because of ridicule. Still, the fear of Middle Easterners so common in America now doesn't exist in Israel—so long as you're a Middle Eastern Jew. If I were Iraqi and Muslim, it might be a problem, given Iraq's threat against Israel. But because I'm Jewish, I'm seen as belonging.

That my connection with Iraq is filtered through a Jewish lens surprises most Americans. When they think of Jews, they think Poland and Germany, bagels and cream cheese, Goldsteins and Rosenbergs. But the first Jews came from Mesopotamia, the land that is today Iraq. They returned to that land in 586 BCE, when the Babylonian Empire conquered and destroyed the Kingdom of Judah—the southern region of ancient Israel. After demolishing the kingdom and leaving it in ruins, the Babylonians took the people of Israel, as captives, again to the land that is today Iraq.

My family remained on the banks of the Tigris and Euphrates rivers for the next 2,500 years until 1950, when the modern Iraqi government forced the Jews to flee as refugees.

With a history like that, Iraqi Jews are as authentically Iraqi and Jewish as you can get. Nonetheless, throughout my life, neither the Jewish nor the Middle Eastern communities have been keen on accepting us fully. In Jewish communities in America, I experienced contempt, ridicule and discrimination based on my heritage and religious traditions. I was expected to subsume my identity in favor of some kind of a pan-Jewish yearning for my European roots. What European roots?

Nor did I have easy entree into the Middle Eastern community of America, which was dominated by Arab Muslims and Christians. I was expected to erase the narrative of my family and community in favor of an anti-Israel, pan-Arab reality. Repeatedly, I received the message that I would be warmly accepted as an Iraqi only if I checked my Jewish identity at the door.

A big part of my desire to go to Israel this time was to return to the place where Mizrahim like me—Jews indigenous to the Middle East and North Africa—are the majority Jewish population, where I do not have to explain my identity or search far and wide for community. Until the mass Russian immigration here in the 1990s, Mizrahim were close to 70 percent of the Jewish population. Now, we are just over half.

I was also eager to visit my elderly Iraqi-Israeli relatives. When they sought refuge in Israel, most of them settled in Ramat Gan, a Tel Aviv suburb. I wanted to get my family's stories on film before it was too late.

I also sought to increase access to film, books, music recordings and other resources of non-European Jews through my organization, the Jewish MultiCultural Project. And I wanted to complete an advanced Hebrew program, so that I could fully immerse myself in the literature of Jews across the globe. In general, I just wanted to be in the place where the international Jewish story would be all around me.

My decision to move here came down to this: love, celebration, and an affirmation of who I am, all of which revolve around life. My reasons not to go involved fear alone—a reason revolving around death. So through the terror and the tears, I chose life. But not until the shores of Tel Aviv appeared on the horizon outside the window of the British Airways jet did I know I had made the right choice. My whole body shook with emotion.

The decision to move to Israel has not gotten any easier in the three months since I arrived for good. Just because I am facing my fears does not mean they are not with me. Only yesterday, I read about people's spinal cords being severed by the shrapnel loaded into suicide bombs. A part of me keeps yelling, "Get out of here and get out of here quick!"

But where else can I live in an apartment building in which Jewish immigrants from Morocco, Iraq, Tunisia, and Iran are all together—and with a Tunisian synagogue directly across the street? With Mizrahi identity reflected in my surroundings, I am free to focus on finding a place within my community, rather than educating strangers over and over about my community's existence. What's more, here I have camaraderie and support for my efforts, instead of having to struggle alone.

I still can pursue the interests I had in the United States—practicing yoga, singing in a rock band, teaching self defense—but now these activities connect me to my community instead of taking me from it. Last week, I taught a self-defense workshop to a group of female teachers at a local school. Half or more of the teachers were Mizrahi. In all the years I offered self-defense workshops in the States, I do not remember even one person of my heritage in the groups.

This is a terrifying and heart-breaking time to be living in Israel. But here I am rooted in the multicultural Jewish story. I can't guarantee that love for my people will be strong enough to keep me here through the daily terror. But for now, this is home.

This piece was excerpted from an article that appeared in *The Washington Post* on February 2, 2003.

Three Yemenite Songs of Women

Translated from the Arabic by Mishael Maswari Caspi

O Daughter, Tell Me

O daughter, tell me your name.
If not, I will ask the shepherd girl.
She said: "Why should I tell you my name?
You cannot afford my dowry anyway…
My price is thirty cows,
Each ready to bear its young;
My price is thirty she-camels,
Whose voices are heard in a forest;
My brideprice is thirty rifles,
And for every rifle a sharp shooter;
My brideprice is thirty fields,
And a worker to water each one;
My brideprice is thirty herds,
With a shepherd for each flock."

Mother, Tell My Father

Mother, tell my father,
Tell him, let him know.
Mother, tell my father,
I don't want to be a shepherd girl.
No more pastures in the mountains,
No more water in the canal,
All the girls have gotten married
But I am still alone.

He Whose Locks Are Black

He whose locks are black,
His hair in braids
Down to his loins.
Tell him, we know him.

His forehead is bright like the moon
In the night's domain

On the night of the fifteenth,
Lighting the darkness.

Hes eyebrows are arched
Like green foliage,
His eyes a goblet
Of grape wine.

His nose is carved like a sword
Shaped to the edge,
His cheeks pure silver,
The work of an artisan.

His smile like lightning shines,
Recognized by all,
His teeth a string of pearls,
Like white dewdrops.

And his neck like a copper vessel,
Oh, how beautiful is the work!
And his chest like the valley of San'a
And its gardens,
Broad enough for horses to gallop
Harnessed in fours.

Reprinted with permission from *Daughters of Yemen*, translated from the Arabic by
Mishael Maswari Caspi (University of California Press, 1985).

Jews of Africa

Jewish in Africa*

Kokasi Keki

Kintu's family lives in a village called Nangolo
Kintu is a teacher
He is reading
Kintu, he counts the days
When six days pass,
he celebrates Shabbat with his family
Naome, our mum, learning to be a cook and caterer
is cooking matoke on a charcoal stove
Kokasi, the first born, is 11, and in P5 class
He helps his mother carry water from the borehole
Katalima, the second born, is 8, in P2 class
She sweeps the room
Deborah, last born, is soon to be three
and walks in and out of nursery class
Deborah sings songs for Chanukah
Today we are celebrating Chanukah
Today, we are going to light seven candles
Katalima lights the candles

*First Prize Winner, 2002 Kulanu International Competition for Young Writers

The author wrote this poem in 2002, when he was 11 years old.

A New Kuzari*

Rabbi Benjamin Z Kreitman

I had the privilege recently to welcome to my office at the World Council of Conservative Judaism Gershom Sizomu, the spiritual leader of the main synagogue of the Abayudaya Jews of Uganda and founder and headmaster of their high school. Gershom and his brother JJ Keki, former chairman of the Abayudaya Jewish community, had come to the States this summer (2001) in part to undergo formal *halachic* conversion. Their community of 600 and more individuals had been observing Judaism since 1919, observing the Sabbath, celebrating the holidays, adhering to *kashrut, shchita, brit* and even *mikveh*. Gershom remained on for another six months to study Judaism intensively at Hebrew Union College, NY, so that he would be able to lead his Jewish community in an appropriate, authentic way.*

This is a remarkable and an amazing story. It is for me a modern replay of the story of the Russian Khazars made famous by Rabbi Yehuda HaLevi in his philosophical tome, the *Kuzari*. The *Kuzari* is based on an historic incident, although in part legend, which tells the story of the king of the Khazars around the 8th century of the Common Era who has a dream wherein the heavenly messenger said to him, "Your intentions are good, but in practice, God is not satisfied with your ways." He thereupon invited representatives of the three faiths, Christianity, Islam and Judaism, to describe their faith, their practices and their celebrations. The wise king of the Khazars discovered that both Christianity and Islam refer back to the Hebrew Bible and validate their religion and their practices by that Bible. He then said to the three representatives: "You authenticate your religion by and through the Jewish Bible. I will therefore accept Judaism as the true faith and I will persuade my people to follow me in this act of conversion." It is told by some historians that the Khazars and their Jewish faith spread over a good part of what is now known as Russia.

In 1919 Christian missionaries traveled to Uganda and sought to convert the "natives" to Christianity. I have the feeling that later on, some Islamic mullahs tried to do the same. The founder of the Abayudaya, like the king of the Khazars, said to the missionaries, "You seek to validate your religion and even to predict the coming of the Messiah on the basis of the Jewish Bible and Jewish tradition. Indeed, you have convinced me to become a Jew." He went through a difficult circumcision and considered himself a Jew and influenced a good number of his community to follow him in the practice of Judaism.

Rabbi Yehuda HaLevi in his subtitle to the *Kuzari* noted that he was writing this tome about the Khazars and their conversion to Judaism to uplift the spirit of the Jews. Sometimes we need the perspective of the outsider or of a stranger to give us a sense of the treasures of Judaism.

Today, we are confronted on the one hand by secular indifference, by the seduction of a materialistic culture, and on the other hand we have the challenges that come from other faiths and other rituals. We need, as in the days of Rabbi Yehuda HaLevi, a perspective on ourselves to see and to behold the meaning of Judaism, the depths of its teachings and the unique way it gives purpose to our lives. The stories of the Ethiopian Jews who with great courage and risk to their lives journeyed to rejoin as Jews their brothers and sisters in the land of Israel is heartwarming. The story of Gershom and JJ and their 600-member congregation in Uganda about to become Halachic Jews* lifts up our spirits and gives us strength and inspiration for the future.

* This essay was written in late 2001. A few months later, a Beit Din traveled to Uganda and officially converted over 300 members of the Abayudaya congregation. Arrangements are being made for another Beit Din to convene there. Gershom Sizomu entered the University of Judaism, Los Angeles, as a rabbinic student in the fall of 2003.

In the Year of Our Joining

Judy Neri

(For JJ Keki and Gershom Sizomu, leaders of the Abayudaya community in Uganda— which had practiced Judaism since 1919—who came to America for a formal conversion in 2001)

You flew between the two skies
the serene blue of the one above
the cloud-clustered one below
You came to the city whose towers
swayed and glinted, huge
in the lower sky after sunset
a place of boxes and angles
so unlike the tree-studded hills
of Uganda crisscrossed by paths
of a human dimension.

In the city the elements took on
new voices; they muttered to themselves
or called out in the asphalt turns
against the iron fist of form.
You found exotic dishes
beyond the fables of the fathers
animals not prized for food
as many books as leaves
in the trees you left behind; the air
filled with words and music
traveling like lightning
in our invisible Tower of Babel

Then one day silver planes
like those you traveled in
crashed into the twin towers
and brought them down
taking with them whole villages
of people, screaming and flailing
through the lower air
to the concrete below
or crushed by the towers' rock

now loosed from its mooring
an avalanche of death

You came looking for ancient truths
in the brave new world even we
who live here inhabit uneasily
You cried with us, shaken
to see familiar death
in so monumental
a guise; you prayed with us as together
we sought comfort and understanding
in the face of all that slithers
beyond understanding
into the coiled snake of madness

In anguish we turned to the old texts
poring over the stories of the first people
to seek the Eternal One, over prayers
worn like pebbles in the streams of your village
by the voices of a thousand years.
Later, when we embraced
and said goodbye, friends become
brothers and sisters, we knew
that the questions would always be larger
than the answers

Rituals in the Bush

Karen Primack

In 1995, following a trip with a Kulanu delegation to the Abayudaya Jews of Uganda, I wrote an article titled "Visiting the Ugandan Miracle." A community faithfully practicing self-taught mainstream Judaism in the middle of "nowhere," having discovered the religion on their own, did seem miraculous. Seven years later, as part of a second delegation charged with a powerful task, I heard Rabbi Joseph Prouser recite the traditional blessing for witnessing a miracle.

Arrival

The delegation arrived at Nabugoye Hill near Mbale, Uganda, on February 5, 2002, to the typical tumultuous Abayudaya musical welcome. We were coming to participate in the *halakhic* conversion of qualified individuals in the 600-member community. The Abayudaya embraced Judaism in 1919 when their leader, Semei Kakungulu, decided to follow only the laws of Moses, which he read about in the Bible that British missionaries had brought to Uganda. The community has been practicing Judaism—and upgrading its knowledge and observance—ever since.

Among us were three rabbis from the US, one rabbi from Israel, a rabbinical student, two musicians, a journalist, two documentary film makers, a horticulturist, and two Kulanu officers. We were welcomed in a long ceremony with speeches and student singing groups performing.

The *Beit Din* was headed by Rabbi Howard Gorin of Tikvat Israel Congregation in Rockville, Maryland, who had converted two Abayudaya leaders, including rabbi Gershom Sizomu, when they were visiting in the US last August. Accompanying Gorin were Prouser, who serves Little Neck Jewish Center in Little Neck, New York; Rabbi Scott Glass of Temple Beth-El in Ithaca, New York; and Rabbi Andrew Sacks, who is a *mohel* (specialist in ritual circumcisions) and Director of the Rabbinical Assembly in Israel. They were joined by Moshe Cotel, then a rabbinical student in New York City who is also a Kulanu board member, and Sizomu.

An initial meeting between the rabbis and the Abayudaya executive committee determined conversion procedures. Two *Batei Din* would convene in the main synagogue and take candidates in family groups, referred by Sizomu based on their observance of Shabbat and *kashrut* (dietary laws). In addition to screening by a *Beit Din*, males—all of whom had been circumcised in the past—would undergo a *hatafat dam brit* (ritual circumcision). Finally, all successful candidates would undergo ritual immersion. Both a nearby river and the community's kosher mikveh, built 70 years ago in the middle of a sugarcane field, would be put to use.

Over the nine-day visit, the rabbinic courts screened over 300 Abayudaya, and the vast majority became officially recognized under Jewish law. Provisions are in place for the rest to complete the conversion process in the near future.

At the Beit Din

Candidates were asked by the rabbis whether they were converting under their own free will, would raise their children as Jews, recognized Adonai as the one and only God, accepted the obligation to observe the *mitzvot* (religious commandments), and whether their children would formally mark their bar and bat mitzvah at the appropriate age. They were also asked to describe the place of Israel in Judaism, and to describe their pattern of religious observance. The rabbis answered questions and counseled candidates about specific family situations. Discussion was punctuated by crowing roosters, a mooing heifer, and distant drumming.

Although most of the candidates had been born into Judaism, there were some exceptions. One 66-year-old woman told the *Beit Din* that she had become interested in Judaism when her Abayudaya boyfriend introduced her to the notion of one God. When she was 15 she and her parents embraced Judaism. One of the rabbis responded, "If you've been practicing Judaism for 50 years, that's good enough for me."

An 80-year-old candidate was the son of the community's first *mohel*. When asked what Judaism's most important teachings are, he replied, "The Ten Commandments and the story of the Exodus, which tells us that God saves his people." Another elder said he had been practicing Judaism since 1920.

Most Abayudaya have biblical names, but those candidates who didn't were given a choice of Hebrew names by the rabbis.

Among the candidates were Israel and Abraham Kakungulu, respectively 76 and 80 years of age, the sons of Semei Kakungulu. Israel reviewed some of the Abayudaya history he recalled. In 1926, when his father Semei was asked the question "What will happen to us?" he prophesied that "the white Jews will come here in airplanes and teach you, so stay firm in your belief."

At one point a side conference occurred over an older man with two wives and two families. Gorin, the *Av Beit Din*, resolved the question citing a precedent used when Yemenite refugees came to Israel in the 1950s. A man would not have to choose between his wives; all would be accepted into Judaism with the proviso that no further bigamous marriages were to occur.

The rabbis said they were moved by the way families have taken on the care of orphans. One young candidate named Moshe appeared before the panel with his younger brother and four orphan boys he is raising.

The *Beit Din* questions and answers continued every day except Shabbat. Answers continued to be impressive. *Why do you want to be part of a persecuted people?* "Because, as my father taught me, this religion is the path to righteousness and God." *What is the essence of Judaism?* "The Ten Commandments, Shabbat, festivals." *Describe one festival.* "On Passover we eat matzah and bitter herbs, and no leaven; it commemorates the Hebrews' slavery in Egypt...."

Eight years ago Sarah, a lifelong Abayudaya in her 30s, named her newborn son Rabin because "I love Israel, so I named my son after the prime minister."

Not all candidates for conversion were accepted by the *Beit Din*. "Some are not prepared, have not studied enough," said Gorin. "We won't pass people simply because they are Abayudaya." The *Beit Din* encouraged them to study, practice, and demonstrate a firm commitment, and predicted that in the future a *Beit Din* could be favorable.

Ritual Immersions

The *mitzvah* of *tevilah* (immersion), which is required for *halakhic* conversions, demands some preparation, especially for women. Nothing should be worn that will interfere with the water touching the skin. Thus jewelry, bandages, and contact lenses are not worn in the mikveh. Also, hair must not be braided, since the water must be able to run through the hair freely.

This last requirement had not reached the Abayudaya in time. Some of the women, in anticipation of this great occasion, had had their hair beautifully braided in salons or by friends. Some of the hairstyles were very elaborate and had required a great deal of time and expense. The rabbis were heartsick about the situation, and it fell upon me to inform the women of the sad news. There were no tears; there was no griping. For many hours, women sat on a mat in Gershom's back yard helping each other unravel the scores of tight, perfect braids.

The ritual immersions were a source of great celebration. On the first of many trips to the nearby river, a group of women and children huddled in the back of the truck belonging to the community's high school. Following a slow ride on tortuous roads in very poor repair, the group faced a long, hilly hike through croplands. Since the path was very narrow, the party proceeded single file in a colorful procession.

Rabbi Scott Glass said in a sermon after his return: "If you think you've seen me in funny situations, you haven't seen anything until you've seen me lowering myself straight down the side of a hill clinging to a banana tree, surrounded by ululating women."

Th4 women crossed the river, wading in their long dresses, and gathered in a secluded spot to disrobe down to their under-slips or colorful sarongs. They removed these under cover of water. A group of 10 or so would enter the water together, but each woman did the immersions and blessings separately and then received applause and ululations from witnesses. Although some of us were prepared to feed the candidates the mikveh blessings word by word, we discovered that all the younger women had memorized the blessings perfectly, and some under-age children insisted on saying the blessings themselves, even though it was a duty of the rabbis.

The rabbis remarked that this had to be a novel chapter in the annals of Jewish history.

Rabbi Andy Sacks, the only mohel, stayed behind at Gershom's house to perform *hatafat dam brit* on all the males who had been passed by a *Beit Din*. This procedure, which requires the drawing of a drop of blood in the area of the circumcision, must be performed before male candidates can undergo immersion.

All male babies born as Abayudaya are circumcised at eight days; those who embrace the religion later are circumcised later. Glass commented in his sermon, "I don't think I will ever forget the line of men and boys snaking down the hill waiting, warily at first, outside the home of Rabbi Gershom. After a short time, however, as each person emerged and assured his fellows that everything was fine and 'it didn't hurt' there would be calls of '*Mazal Tov!*' to each who completed the 'ordeal.'"

A Torah and Other Gifts

The delegation brought many gifts, but the greatest was a Sefer Torah that Rabbi Gorin delivered. His congregation donated $6000 for the purchase of this kosher Torah for the Abayudaya. (Rabbi Menachem Youlis of Silver Spring, Maryland, had donated his services as a scribe in reconditioning the Torah.)

The Torah was dedicated in a moving ceremony during which a group of Abayudaya approached the center of the synagogue yard carrying their older, borrowed Torah, singing psalms and prayers in Luganda, the local language. The visitors approached in a group from the opposite direction, carrying the new Torah and singing Hebrew songs, led by singer/songwriter Laura Wetzler with her guitar. The two groups joined in a noisy and joyful procession and circled the sanctuary seven times, carrying the Torahs under a *huppah* (wedding canopy). Torah portions were chanted by Gorin in Hebrew and by Gershom in Luganda. The entire congregation joined in the singing of "Hatikvah," which even the children seemed to know.

Deep Questions on Shabbat

On Shabbat eve, visitors attended services in the main synagogue on Nabugoye Hill, which was lit by candlelight (the community has virtually no electricity). The Kabbalat Shabbat service featured beautiful singing in Hebrew and Luganda, included, of course, the now-famous Abayudaya melody for "*L'cha Dodi*," featured on their commercial recording. Kiddush was held at the home of Gershom Sizomu and his wife Tziporah Naisi, who made excellent challah over a flame (they have no oven), followed by an intimate dinner for the guests—chapati, white beans, matoke (plantains), cooked greens, and a chicken slaughtered according to Jewish law by Gershom. Glass commented, "I haven't spent 10 minutes here that weren't extraordinary."

Shabbat morning services were even more high-spirited than usual on the Shabbat the *Beit Din* visited, in part because many of the Abayudaya had already been fully converted. The concept of the *aufruf* was explained, and Gershom and Tziporah approached the Torah and received a special blessing because their wedding would be in the coming week. The concept became popular immediately, and six other couples crowded onto the bimah for a second *aufruf*. Now their weddings would also occur in the coming week.

During the afternoon, rabbis and congregants engaged in informal teaching sessions. The rabbis expressed surprise and delight at the depth and complexity of the questions. For example, someone asked why the 5th commandment in Exodus begins with the words *Zakhor Et Yom HahSabbat*...("Remember the

Sabbath day") while that in Deuteronomy begins *Shamor Et Yom Ha Shabbat* ("Observe/keep the Sabbath day").

Seven Brides

The final two days of the visit were devoted to *huppah* ceremonies for the community's already-married leaders.

On the first wedding day, Gershom and Tziporah were united in a traditional Jewish ceremony with all four rabbis officiating. Glass adapted the opening words (*Baruchim habaim*) to an African melody. The chief officiant was Gorin, but the *ketubah* (wedding contract) was read by Prouser in Aramaic and English. The *Sheva Brachot* (Seven Blessings) were chanted by Cotel, Prouser, Sacks and Glass. For the first time in history—so we believe—an Abayudaya *hatan* (groom) in Uganda smashed a glass with his foot to commemorate the destruction of the Temples in Jerusalem.

The following day saw the separate weddings of six couples. Wedding dresses for the brides were purchased by Kulanu. We explained that providing for a bride is a *mitzvah,* and that the *mitzvah* would be extended if these dresses were freely lent out to future brides in the community. It was my special privilege to spend an unforgettable morning shopping with brides. Each selected a special *kitenge* with embroidery or other trim or detailing.

The participants, all Abayudaya leaders, read like a biblical Who's Who: Aaron was wed to Naomi, Joab to Miriam, Enosh to Shirah, Samson to Dinah, Uri to Zerida, and Moses to Esther. Each couple had a separate ceremony, complete with the reading of the *ketubah* in Aramaic (sometimes with Luganda or English translation) and chanting of the Seven Blessings

The *huppah* had been made from a white tallit supported by four long stalks of fresh sugarcane. After the final ceremony, the poles were hacked into pieces and distributed to children to savor the sweetness of the occasion. This wonderful new tradition should be adopted in all Jewish communities where sugarcane is available!

Closure

At a formal farewell meeting, Keki exclaimed, "Three-quarters of world Jewry now recognizes us!"

Rabbi Sacks observed: "I have never had the experience of trying to teach children when they are hungry and malnourished. I don't have a concept of sharing these things when people are just trying to survive." Most Abayudaya live, as their neighbors do, in mud huts with no electricity or running water. Annual per capita income has been estimated at $600.

Rabbi Glass encouraged the community to realize the great value of their own traditions and to continue to develop their own melodies and sing Psalms in Luganda. Glass urged the community to "retain a special imprint on Jewish practice, as every community in the Jewish Diaspora has done."

None of the rabbis had been to Africa before, but all are anxious to return. It must have been the winning combination of the warm weather, fresh air, and deep spirituality of the Abayudaya.

We Are Grieving for Sarah Nantabo

Rabbi J. Hershy Worch

Sarah Nantabo is dead ... we are grieving. Who can fathom the depths of a Jewish heart? Who can write a eulogy for the soul of a leader among the Abayudaya, a mother, a daughter?

AAAAAaaaaiiiiiiieeeee

I have tasted her oversweet-cha, eaten her delicious matoke, listened to her chanting the sacred liturgy of her people, our people, and watched her checking, grain by grain, kilos of rice for traces of bugs which might render the food she cooked unkosher. She was our sister.

The loss of Sarah Nantabo is our loss.

All women of the Abayudaya have beauty and grace, but Sarah was gifted with an abundance of rare talents and genuine charisma.

AN ELEGY ON SUDDEN DEATH

Shall I tell them of your blue black hair?
and you crumpled like a leaf.
Talk joy of you, let them share?
and you gone beyond belief.
The shy glad smile, would they care?
and you gone God-knows where.

Shall I tell them of your classic face?
gurgling laughter, the time we had.
Describe your skin, lips and breath?
or the manner of your death.
Herein and thereinafter
forever in that other place
where you've been had.

The death of Sarah Nantabo rocks our firmament whether we find ourselves in the USA or in Australia or in Africa.

The biggest smile in the world has died.

Ma Nishtana in Luganda

Translated by Gershom Sizomu
Compiled by Murray F. Spiegel and Rickey Stein

Lwakyi ekyiro kyino kyanjawulo kubiro ebilala byonna?
Mubiro ebilala byonna tulya emigati emizimbulukuse oba egitali
mizimbulukuse; mukyiro kyino tulya emigati egitali mizimbulukuse zokka.
Mubiro ebilala byonna tulya enva zonna zonna; mukyiro kyino tulya enva
ezikawa zokka.
Mubiro ebilala byonna tetukoza omulundi nogumu; mukyiro kyino tukoza
emirundi ebiri. Mubiro ebilala byonna tulya tutudde oba nga tweganzise;
mukyiro kyino tulya tweganzise.

Why is this night different from all other nights?
On all other nights we may eat either leavened or unleavened bread, but on
this night only unleavened bread.
On all other nights we may eat any species of herbs, but on this night only
bitter herbs. On all other nights we do not dip even once, but on this night
we dip twice.
On all other nights we eat either sitting or reclining, but on this night we
all recline.

The Escape

Rose Bromberg

The women bring their laundry down to the stream. Their daughters follow in procession, forming a line in order of their age and size. The laundry is placed in large, coiled baskets; then the women balance the baskets on their heads as they walk barefoot down to the water's edge.

One of the older girls wades up to her calves and washes the clothing with soap. She takes a shirt and, using her hands, she scrubs one side of the shirt against the other in the water. Then she rinses it and brings it back to the basket. She instructs the younger girls to do the same. They learn by watching, listening, and helping one another. When they finish, they place the laundry back into their coiled baskets and once again balance them on their heads. The women hang the clothes outside on a line near their *tukels*.

The women then go inside their *tukels*. The twigs, mud, and straw from which the *tukels* are made help keep out the heat. Surrounding their homes, there are fields for their crops and pastures for the livestock, most of which are goats and sheep. You may see a horse or two. Cattle and mules roam free. This part of the country, near the Semien Mountains, does get rain. After a long rain, the grass becomes green and tall. Flowers, trees, and berry bushes grow. But people can starve and die from poverty, diseases, displacement, civil wars, and clashes with the Church.

Most of these people are farmers. In addition, the women cook, sew, make decorative and household pottery, and take care of the children and domestic animals. They also make colorful baskets. From metal, the men form knives and plows. Even jewelry. And they weave cloth and tan skins. These people have a tribal name—the Beta Israel. Some call them *Falasha*, but this means stranger or outcast and is considered a derogatory term. For 3,000 years the Beta Israel observed the Torah, the Sabbath, and Jewish festivals.

It is against the law for the Beta Israel and others to leave Ethiopia. The Church takes over synagogues and confiscates Hebrew books. Marriages are arranged for the youngsters of the Beta Israel, as is the local custom. They are rich if they have a mule to carry their load and a horse to pull their cart. There were times when soldiers stormed through their village, burned their *tukels*, stole their food and water, and even executed people. But the Beta Israel remain faithful to the Torah. Their reward is Jerusalem.

Today, one of the women can't go down to the stream to launder her family's clothes. According to the customs of the Beta Israel, today this woman must sit in the *Margam Bet*. There may be other women already in this hut who have started their "monthly bleeding." They aren't allowed to work or touch food, but they can wander through the village. Other women come to feed them as the members of the hut sit, laughing and talking. But no laundry is washed by these women. And no other work is performed by them. If they have daughters, their daughters will complete the task.

The atmosphere is filled with tension. Sometimes, missionaries come to the Beta Israel and try forcefully to make them accept the cross. Some Beta Israel did convert to Christianity. Others said that they will remain true to their religion, but then they were killed. Many people believe that the Jewish population brings the *buda* (evil eye). Translation: the diseases and bad things that happen to us are here because of the Beta Israel and the Jews.

After the Beta Israel children walk home from school, other children from nearby villages lie in wait for them, calling them names, and beating them. Parents are scared. Children are scared.

Some don't believe that it will get worse, but one family decides it's time to leave. That day, mother and daughter go to the stream, balancing their baskets of laundry on their heads. The mother walks down. Then she quickly steps into the water, washes the clothing, and returns to her *tukel* with her daughter. There is much to do before nightfall.

Gannet washes herself in the stream, then collects water in her jug. She walks back to her *tukel* and wraps some food, including the flat, round *injera*. She uses it to scoop up the spicy vegetables and juices when her mother cooks *shiro wett*. Her mother, Almaz, packs the food on the mule. They will leave some *zamed* and loved ones behind.

Getu is leaving, too. He lives in the next *tukel* and is only 8 years old, a couple of years younger than Gannet. He has no siblings or parents, only a grandmother whom he must leave behind. He says goodbye to his grandmother, knowing he will never see her again. As he kisses her, his grandmother's eyes moisten with tears. "May you arrive safely," she prays.

As Getu begins to walk out of the *tukel*, his grandmother motions for him to put out his hand. She places several *birr* in his palm. "These are my savings. Hide them in your clothing and when you need a coin, take one out to bribe people along the way. There may be *shiftas* who will try to steal your belongings. Others may try to hurt you because you try to escape. Give them *birr* and hope they go away. You will also pay the guide."

The group leaves at nightfall. "*Tenastyilin*," they say to greet their guide.

"*Tenastyilin*," the guide responds.

He instructs them that they must walk north toward the Semien Mountains, then go west and cross into the Sudan. There they will find the refugee camp and eventually be taken to Israel. It will take them several weeks to arrive, depending on weather conditions, availability of food and water, disease, and other obstacles.

They walk until night falls again. It's chilly. The guide makes a small fire before they sleep. Some Beta Israel sleep on the ground. Some of them make beds out of the branches of trees. It begins to drizzle. Gannet is cold and reaches for her *shammas* to wrap around her. As she turns, the branches crackle.

"Shh!" whispers her mother. "We must be quiet! If we make noise we may be noticed. Maybe tomorrow we will be lucky enough to meet people who will give us shelter."

They keep moving. In mud and across flat lands. Through hills and steep mountains. Some don't have shoes or sandals to wear. They have thorns in their feet and wear only their torn and tattered clothes on their backs. Their food and water run out.

They pass a small town. Gannet says, "I will walk through the town to see what I can find for us." Before she leaves, she wraps part of her *shammas* around her face so she won't be recognized or attacked by strangers.

Getu goes to look for berries and grass to eat. He collects water from a nearby stream. After lunch, Almaz begins to feel ill. She doubles over in pain.

"Mama!" shouts Gannet, "what is wrong?"

"I am sick. I can't go on," she responds. "Leave me here."

The group can't wait but Gannet won't leave without her mother. She tells the guide, "Take Getu and go without us. I will stay here with my mother."

The guide responds, "You don't know how to take care of yourselves. We will wait a little longer."

Almaz is pale and weak. She can't sit up. They give Almaz time to rest. Then they carry her part of the way. Realizing how close they are to losing Almaz, all of them pray briefly, "We the living shall bless the Lord forevermore...."

The Beta Israel continue to walk and move on. Sometimes they walk at night before the sun rises. Other times, they walk during the day under an intense, burning sun.

They stop again at dusk and they rest near a village. Before deciding whether or not they will stay here for the night, the guide walks around the village to see if it's safe. A tall man comes out of his *tukel*, watching. He is aiming a gun at the guide.

"What do you want?" he asks. He tightly holds his gun and his gaze never leaves the guide.

"I am here with my family," answers the guide. "We are Ethiopians and are on our way to visit relatives. We have no more food or water. We are hoping to stop here for the night."

The man eyes him suspiciously. He asks, "Where are you going?"

The guide gives him the name of a nearby village.

The man steps back, lowers his gun, and says, "You may stay with us for the night."

The guide thanks him and Almaz, Gannet, and Getu join the man and his family in their *tukel*. After dinner, the guide collects *birr* from Almaz and Getu. He wants to pay the man in exchange for some food and water to take with them the next day.

Almaz and Gannet sleep inside the *tukel* with the man's family. The guide and Getu sleep outside the *tukel* because there is no room inside for them.

Almaz and Gannet rise early the next morning. They thank the family, and go outside. Getu is just waking up, but the guide is gone. So is most of their food and water. They realize the guide took their last *birr* and isn't returning.

They must make the rest of the journey by themselves. They continue to walk ... and walk ... and walk.

All of a suddden, Getu sees something move in the bushes. Then he hears a roar. In his surprise, he points and says, "A lion!" Everyone freezes. Almaz wrings her hands together. Gannet's eyes are wide with fear. No one makes a sound. They walk silently away from the sounds of the lion and into safety.

"How do we know we are walking in the right direction?" asks Gannet. Her mother answers, "By the rising and setting of the sun, we will find the Sudan. We will walk west."

Many insects bite. The Beta Israel make flyswatters to try and keep the insects away. They begin to see plateaus. Then the plant life and vegetation change. They see frogs, crocodiles, worms, and snakes. They continue on.

Getu thinks of the Sudan. "Do you think we will make it?" he asks Almaz. She responds softly but firmly, "We will make it. The trip is difficult for everyone."

Their skin blisters from the sun. The sand blows in their faces. At night, they sneak past the guards and cross the border into the Sudan. Finally, they reach the refugee camp. Almaz lays on the ground. She is very weak and may die. Gannet and Getu suffer, too.

A relief agency worker who is also a translator comes over to them. He is a nice young man with a pleasant face. "We need to get some information from you," he says. He gives each one of them a registration card. The date of their arrival and the number of the hut they will stay in is printed on it. Almaz, Gannet, and Getu will need to show this card to get their food rations and water. After a few minutes, the relief worker calls to a nurse.

She comes over and introduces herself. "My name is Sandy." She motions for Almaz to sit up, make a fist with her hand, and put her arm out in a straight line. Almaz lifts her arm but it feels so heavy. Sandy treats

Almaz by giving her some medicine and water through an intravenous (IV). As Sandy inserts the needle into Almaz's vein, Almaz winces. Sandy then gives the rest of the group IVs, water, and some pills to swallow.

"Call me if you need anything," she offers in English, looking around for the translator.

Gannet knows a little English. She asks Sandy, pointing to others in need of care, "Who are these other people?"

"They are Christians and Moslems who are refugees. They are in need of help, too. People are dying everywhere. I need to go open more boxes of food and medicine. I'll be back later to check on you."

They stay there that night, sleeping in a hut. They share the hut with several strangers. Sandy returns to check on them. She tells another relief worker, "Almaz needs more medicine. Unfortunately, there are problems. Some of the supplies don't reach us. There aren't enough trucks, roads are blocked, and we can't keep up with all the people coming. Let's try our best and see what we can do."

Almaz doesn't get her medicine for another three days. During that time, she gets much weaker. Friday evening comes. "What should we do for the Sabbath?" asks Getu.

Gannet warns, "I heard that Jews were being beaten by other refugees. It is too risky to pray."

But after dark, they greet the Sabbath. In barely a whisper, they murmur to one another,

"*Sanbat salam.*"

All of them need more medicine, food, and water. Gannet sees another refugee acting strangely around them. She's afraid that this person may report them for escaping Ethiopia. They don't take any chances. None of them will leave the hut to get their medicine or food ration.

That night, they go to sleep early. It's dark. Gannet wakes up. She hears a sound outside. A sound like rustling. "It's just a bird or animal," she thinks to herself. Then she hears low voices. She looks at Almaz and sees that she's sleeping deeply. Getu is sleeping but looks restless, as if the sounds and voices are beginning to wake him.

Gannet lies still and pulls her sheet up close to her neck. Suddenly, there is a crash. Gannet moves to Getu and covers his mouth with her hand. By this time he's up and she doesn't want him to make any sounds. Then all is silent.

The next morning they meet another refugee from Ethiopia. He explains, "Last night, we had *shiftas* come through our camp. They tried to steal our water and valuables. Luckily, no one was hurt."

Another few days pass by. Almaz slowly gains strength. Gannet and Getu are more resilient. With the help of the medicine, they are strong enough to make the trip to Israel.

They learn more about the rescue operation and airlift. They may need to wait for exit permits and visas. Finally, they are told to get ready to leave the refugee camp. The bus comes to take them to the plane. Many others are there, waiting. There is fighting to get onto the bus. Some refugees will be turned away if there isn't enough room.

As the bus arrives on the field, Getu exclaims, "That is the strangest bird I have ever seen!" For the first time, he sees a plane. After boarding, they hear a voice: "You are part of Operation Moses...people from all over the world have been collecting money for you and helping to plan your escape from Ethiopia...." They land in Europe where they transfer to another plane which takes them to Israel.

Almaz is immediately taken to a nearby hospital. Getu and Gannet go to an absorption center. They are happy to sleep in a comfortable and clean bed.

After the first night in Israel, Gannet and Getu wake up. Gannet sees that Getu looks a little sad. She asks him, "Getu, what is wrong?"

He replies, "I am thinking of my grandmother. I hope she is well and isn't worrying about me."

"Me, too," says Gannet. "I am thinking of my mother. I will visit her in the hospital. I had dreams about all of us last night. I wonder about my aunts and uncles at home."

Getu then goes into the bathroom. He plays with the shower by turning the knob on and off. "Gannet," he yells, "look! Come feel the hot and cold water!"

A volunteer comes to speak with them and gives them medicine, fresh towels, new clothes, and more food. Gannet looks at her new dress. She sees the zipper and opens it and closes it, opens it and closes it. She feels so good to be clean and in new clothes!

There's food on the table. Getu picks up a potato and drinks some tea. After eating half of the potato, he can't eat anymore.

Gannet decides to eat a hard-boiled egg with a slice of bread. As the volunteer proceeds to crack and peel the egg, Gannet picks up a piece of bread. It's a funny shape: almost a square. And it's very soft and thick. One piece has a few small seeds on top. She bites into the bread. Then she inspects the seeds, removes each one, and eats them separately. She thinks they have a funny taste, but she likes it. Certainly different from the *injera* she ate in Ethiopia!

Gannet and Getu must recuperate from the trip and from their illnesses. They will go to "homes," perhaps kibbutzim, hotel rooms or other places to learn skills or go to school. It will take time for them to adjust to this new life.

Epilogue:

Many refugees were saved in "Operation Moses", which airlifted the Beta Israel to Israel, but there were more who couldn't come. Later, there was "Operation Solomon" which tried to get the rest of the Beta Israel out of Ethiopia. Since 1990, the Ethiopian government has allowed the remainder of the refugees to leave the country, but Israel is placing restrictions on their immigration. This is an area of great controversy for Jews everywhere.

Glossary:

tukels - round mud huts
Beta Israel - Literally, House of Israel (refers to the Ethiopian Jews)
Margam Bet - House of Blood or Women's Hut
buda - evil eye
injera - round, flat bread
shiro wett - spicy vegetable stew
zamed - relatives
birr - coins
shiftas - bandits
tenastyilin - hello (in Amharic)
shammas - scarf
Sanbat salam - good Shabbos

Teaching and Learning in Sefwi Wiawso

Margie Klein

I stood in a clay hut with blank walls, the heat dense on my skin, the scent of red peppers and farm animals sifting through my nostrils. In front of me sat 10 Ghanaian farmers lined up on wooden benches too low to the ground for their size, looking up at me for guidance and inspiration. It was my second day in Sefwi Wiawso, Ghana, where I had been sent for a month as a Kulanu volunteer to help the community think about agricultural development and foster Jewish learning. Needless to say, the task of incorporating the twin goals of agriculture and Jewish education into a lasting and unified Jewish understanding was daunting, but on this day, my first worry was getting through an hour and a half of class without running out of material.

After teaching the group some songs, I extracted from my out-of-place New York bag what would be my primary learning aid, a book called *Let the Earth Teach You Torah*, Teva's teaching guide about Judaism and the environment. With the help of community member Kofi Kwateng as translator, I read the group a quote from Abraham Joshua Heschel about *brachot* (blessings). The passage asserts that we repeat *brachot* all the time to remind ourselves of the holiness in the world, that everyday things we do should be appreciated as miracles. As Kofi translated the quotation to the engrossed group, I considered Heschel's position. "That sounds nice," I thought, "but what New Yorker is going to see the holiness of boarding the subway, or buying apples from the infinite fruit supply at Stop n Shop? It is hard enough to get anyone to think about this stuff once a week in synagogue."

Interrupting my thoughts, Joseph Armah raised his hand to comment. "What the rabbi says is true," Joseph said. "You must always thank God. God makes all things possible."

"Yes," added Samuel Mintah, "God must be on your mind all the time. You must always thank Him, and ask Him to help keep your faith strong. Praise God!"

"Hallelujah!" answered the rest of the room.

"He makes the corn grow. Praise God!"

"Hallelujah!"

"He gives us children. Praise God!"

"Hallelujah!"

As other members of the class joined in enthusiastically affirming that God was central and blessing God was obvious, I came to a realization that would grow throughout my trip and shape my experience in ways I never anticipated: These people have a whole lot more to teach me about Judaism than I have to give them.

True, I know Hebrew and Jewish ritual; I know how to fix a good bagel brunch and Shabbas dinner party. True too, perhaps more important, I know to try to treat people with respect and dignity, and to fight for the causes I believe in. Yet often I don't know how to pray. Often I don't feel a connection to nature, or understand the powerful role that connection played in the lives of Jews who came before me. Often I don't remember to give thanks or to step back in awe. The Jews of Sefwi Wiawso do.

After this first lesson, I came to see my role in the community as a transmitter of Jewish teachings that can inform the decisions we make about agricultural development. I could find the texts, but I trusted the community to use the power of its faith in the direct relevance of the Torah and Talmud to interpret the texts into action. So when we read the Talmudic lesson of *ba'al tashchit,* which instructs that even in war one must not cut down a fruit tree, and by extension in times of peace one should not destroy anything useful in nature, the community committed itself to principles of sustainable agriculture, and agreed to explore ways to learn about organic farming. With my help, the community was able to secure a yearlong training program in sustainable agriculture run by the UN Food and Agriculture program, and hopes to use their new knowledge to make their community farm successful. Throughout their process of deciding how to attain help and how to divide up community land, the community always came back to the text, and considered how Jewish teachings could guide their decisions.

Coming home, I am about to start a career as an environmental organizer, working to make corporations and governments more accountable to regular citizens, to live out the Jewish values in which I've come to believe. In my work, I will remember the texts I studied in Ghana and the ease with which the community took them in. I will remember that it is possible to be both reverent and practical, to embrace Jewish tradition and progressive vision. In Sefwi Wiawso, they prove this possibility every day.

The High Seas*

Carolivia Herron

Grandma Ernestine's Friday night candles light the way to the high seas. It is her mother, my Great Grandmother Olivia, who whispers the story to me when I am nine years old and she is 103 years old.

"Can you tell me about slavery when you were a little girl?"

"Slavery? I was there, you know, down near Norfolk near the fishing boats, that's where we lived when the word came that the colored folks were free. I was standing just outside the house and I heard all the clapping and crying for joy. I could hear them all along the bushes and in the back. A man came and read the paper, it wasn't far from the front of my house. Then he said that meant there were no slaves no more. And people were dancing and singing but they didn't want to sing too loud for fear the white folks would hear them. They went back to the huts so white folks couldn't hear them so happy."

"And how did you feel, Grandma, you were a little girl like me, weren't you glad to be free from slavery?"

But then she got the most awful look on her face, her face screwed up like a piece of wrinkled black crepe paper with two bright blue jewels shining out, her terrifying bright blue eyes. I thought she was going to spit on me.

"You stupid idiot, don't you know?"

"Know what, Grandma?" I could hardly form the words. She had never been angry with me before. But she started to turn away from me like I was too stupid to talk to any more. She groaned up from her chair and turned to go upstairs just leaving me standing there.

"Grandma?" I could barely whisper.

But just as she turned to go up the stairs she stopped. She was silent for a moment. What was she thinking? I suspect, at 103 years old, she said to herself, "If I don't tell someone now, when am I going to tell someone?"

So she turned around and looked at me just standing there.

"Olivia chile, Carol, Oscar's baby, don't you know we were never slaves? We were free Negroes all those slavery years.

She sat down and started talking to me.

"We hated the white folks, we hated the slavery, but we weren't slaves. How come you don't know that? We came up slow from the Georgia Islands, fishing our way up. It took us a hundred years to get from Georgia to Portsmouth, Virginia. We were fishermen, all of us, and we paid the white folks a part of what we earned so they would leave us alone. I hate them, the white folks, they gave us a hard time."

(By the way, this great grandmother who hated white folks married and cherished a white Irishman, but it was clear that she didn't consider him white. It seems the Irish were so low in the scale of things that this black skinned woman could marry an Irishman without violating the miscegenation laws. My grandmother grew up as Irish and Black, and sent St. Patrick's day presents to me at college to the stunned surprise of the white folks there.)

"Girl, let me tell you. We come from a pirate who landed in Tripoli, Africa, and he married a Jewish woman they stole from Europe somewhere."

There was a pirate ship where the sailors earned their living by stealing Jews from North Mediterranean countries, carried them across to North Africa, and ransomed them for gold and jewels in the Jewish communities of the South Mediterranean.

"My great grandfather was one of these pirates," she said. She told me that our family was a free black family that had been founded on one of the Georgia Sea Islands by this Portuguese pirate great grandfather and a Jewish woman from Spain. "The Jewish family had moved from Spain to Portugal, and then somewhere else over there, I don't know which country, except it was on the Mediterranean Sea. Maybe it was even Italy. Wherever it was, she thought of herself as Spanish and Portuguese. Then she was stolen from one of those Mediterranean countries." She told me the Portuguese pirate fell in love with one of the captured Jewish women. They jumped ship together in North Africa, in Tripoli, and came to America, to the Georgia Sea Islands, on one of the first United States Marine ships, and started a family.

Their children intermarried with the Sea Islanders. Grandma Olivia told me, "We're Geechees, a mixture of African and Portuguese from the islands off Georgia." Black Geechees. I did not even know that Geechees were a real group of people. I thought it was a pet name of endearment because my mother often told me with a smile that I am a Geechee. "You and your father are both Geechees," she would say, and hold me close with love. I found out later in books and movies that "geechee" was sometimes used as an insult for wild blacks who lived away from everybody and had not been slaves. Even later I discovered that Geechees are a real group of people living on the Georgia Sea Islands, near the Gullahs.

He stole her. He changed his mind. Sailing the high seas. And she came with him. My Great Grandmother Olivia told me they fell in love with each other. They left the world into which they had been born and moved somewhere else.

They are both nameless in our oral tradition, but she has leaned through history to tell me that her name is Sarah bat Asher. I thank you, Sarah, my Great Grandmother Olivia's Great Grandmother. From generation to generation you are the one who has sent me the Shabbat candles.

*© 2003 by Carolivia Herron.

"The High Seas" is excerpted from *Peacesong*, the story of the author's path toward embracing her Judaism and her current work in progress.

A Jew Approved by Hashem

Hadassah W. Harr-Ell

Hey, you there with skin so dark
Why are you wearing that outlandish frock
With handmade fringes on the border
You, my friend, are out of order!!

Who are you, to tell me what to wear?
Can't I be accepted here,
 a different Jew?

No, because you're not the right shade,
What are you doing here anyway, spade?
Since when do they look like you?
So, go stand in the other line
Until we decide to give you the sign
Of RECOGNITION! [That you are one of the Chosen Few]

But I, too, am a Jew,
Every bit as much as you,
So it is not hard for me to
accept you as my brother.

I am not a brother of yours.
If really Jewish, the clothes you wore
Would look like those from my country.

But I was not born where you were, brother,
I am a Jew from a different culture,
I don't care what you wear.
So, what's all this I hear?
Your dress, your clothes--I accept you.
So who are you to say I'm not a Jew?

Since I know I'M Jewish, I'm the one to say,
Maybe by measuring your DNA .
It is nothing to worry about, just a test—
Let me think, maybe not the best—

Delancey Synagogue in New York City
Might find this technique blasphemy.
Even there a member died
Who was a Nazi, certified,
And no one knew it! So you're right,
Who am I to say with water-tight
Certainty if you are a Jew. Forget that test
Never mind the clothing and all the rest.
Here are your stamped documents;
Accept them with my compliments:
A JEW APPROVED BY HASHEM.

Thanks HASHEM for your intervention,
and may all of us Jews without pretension
accept each other regardless of differences.
Let's take down all those fences!

Jewish Life in Namibia

Lucy Y. Steinitz

When someone needs to say Kaddish in Namibia, they usually start phoning on Friday afternoons. "Can you come to services tonight?" they ask. Our recently Bar-Mitzvahed son, Sergio, who was born in Guatemala and converted as an infant, is the only one in our family who qualifies. My daughter and I invariably lament: Why, in this community that has dwindled down to fewer than twenty affiliated families, do they still stick stubbornly to the Orthodox tradition of only counting men? There is nobody left who is still *shomer-Shabbos* (keeping of all the commandments for the Sabbath), and the nearest kosher store lies more than 1000 miles away. (For Passover, we have to order our matzoh six weeks in advance—and then pray that it gets here). So, why bother?

But stubbornness and tradition are what this community is all about. The synagogue was built in 1924 and once served 120 families. Most left around the time of Namibia's independence from South Africa in 1990. But almost miraculously, some Jewish families still trickle in—an airline pilot who works for a subsidiary of South African Airways, a translator at the local French embassy, or a family like ours who came more than five years ago as temporary development workers (in education and HIV/AIDS) and fell so in love with the country that we are now permanent residents. Festive occasions also include the Honourable Minister of Labour (who spent many years interned in Robbin Island with Nelson Mandela, and is now married to a Jewish woman and helps raise their two daughters as Jews), as well as one of the world's best-known gem specialists, "Old Man Saul Pieters," for whom the uniquely marbled brown-and-blue Pietersite is aptly named.

Long-time residents also include entrepreneurs, a few ex-commercial farmers, Holocaust survivors, some professionals, and others—all of whom were once upon a time drawn to this vast and arid landscape, with its small population and promises of better times ahead. But are those promises still valid? On the one hand, the community is investing money to renovate the synagogue for worship and social functions. On the other, it is hiring a historian to interview our elders before it is too late, thus ensuring that we shall, at the very least, have more than our cemeteries to document that our community once existed.

As for our family, we have made our compromises. Never before in my life would I have imagined sitting behind a *mechitsa* (the division that separates the men and women) week after week, enduring the frustrations of unequal participation in the synagogue. Yet I come regularly, undeterred.

There are many advantages to living in Namibia, especially in the opportunities for *tikun olam* (repairing the world). And sometimes one finds other compensations as well. My favorite story comes from a group of nuns in the far north of Namibia, whom I visit regularly through my work in HIV/AIDS. One evening at dinner, one of the religious sisters popped the question:

"Which church do YOU belong to, Dr. Lucy?" she asked.

"I belong to a synagogue," I answered, matter-of-factly. "It's a Jewish church, in Windhoek (Namibia's capital)."

"You're JEWISH?" responded the nun, her jaw dropping. "And was your mother Jewish too?"

"Yes," I answered. "As far back as our family can remember, our family has been Jewish."

Suddenly there was silence, as all the nuns looked at me anew. "Oh," said the first one, extending her arms in embrace: "Then you must be a relative of Jesus!"

Jews of Asia

Kimchee on the Seder Plate

Rabbi Angela Warnick Buchdahl

One year my mother put kimchee, a spicy, pickled cabbage condiment, on our seder plate. My Korean mother thought it was a reasonable substitution since both kimchee and horseradish elicit a similar sting in the mouth, the same clearing of the nostrils. She also liked kimchee on gefilte fish and matza. "Kimchee just like *maror*, but better," she said. I resigned myself to the fact that we were never going to be a "normal" Jewish family.

I grew up part of the "mixed multitude" of our people: an Ashkenazi Reform Jewish father, a Korean Buddhist mother. I was born in Seoul and moved to Tacoma, Washington, at the age of five. Growing up, I knew my family was atypical, yet we were made to feel quite at home in our synagogue and community. My Jewish education began in my synagogue preschool, extended through cantorial and rabbinical school at Hebrew Union College (HUC), and continues today. I was the first Asian American to graduate from the rabbinical program at HUC, but definitely not the last—a Chinese American rabbi graduated the very next year, and I am sure others will follow.

As a child, I believed that my sister and I were the "only ones" in the Jewish community—the only ones with Asian faces, the only ones whose family trees didn't have roots in Eastern Europe, the only ones with kimchee on the seder plate. But as I grew older, I began to see myself reflected in the Jewish community. I was the only multiracial Jew at my Jewish summer camp in 1985; when I was a song-leader a decade later, there were a dozen. I have met hundreds of people in multiracial Jewish families in the Northeast through the Multiracial Jewish Network. Social scientist Gary Tobin numbers interracial Jewish families in the hundreds of thousands in North America.

As I learned more about Jewish history and culture, I found it very powerful to learn that being of mixed race in the Jewish community was not just a modern phenomenon. We were a mixed multitude when we left Egypt and entered Israel, and the Hebrews continued to acquire different cultures and races throughout our Diaspora history. Walking through the streets of modern-day Israel, one sees the multicolored faces of Ethiopian, Russian, Yemenite, Iraqi, Moroccan, Polish, and countless other races of Jews—many facial particularities, but all Jewish. Yet, if you were to ask the typical secular Israeli on the street what it meant to be Jewish, she might respond, "It's not religious so much, it's my culture, my ethnicity."

115

If Judaism is about culture, what then does it mean to be Jewish when Jews come from so many different cultures and ethnic backgrounds?

As the child of a non-Jewish mother, a mother who carried her own distinct ethnic and cultural traditions, I came to believe that I could never be "fully Jewish" since I could never be "purely" Jewish. I was reminded of this daily: when fielding the many comments like, "Funny, you don't look Jewish," or having to answer questions on my halakhic status as a Jew. My internal questions of authenticity loomed over my Jewish identity throughout my adolescence into early adulthood, as I sought to integrate my Jewish, Korean, and secular American identities.

It was only in a period of crisis, one college summer while living in Israel, that I fully understood what my Jewish identity meant to me. After a painful summer of feeling marginalized and invisible in Israel, I called my mother to declare that I no longer wanted to be a Jew. I did not look Jewish, I did not carry a Jewish name, and I no longer wanted the heavy burden of having to explain and prove myself every time I entered a new Jewish community. She simply responded by saying, "Is that possible?" It was only at that moment that I realized I could no sooner stop being a Jew than I could stop being Korean, or female, or me. I decided then to have a *giyur*, what I termed a reaffirmation ceremony, in which I dipped in the *mikveh* and reaffirmed my Jewish legacy. I have come to understand that anyone who has seriously considered her Jewish identity struggles with the many competing identities that the name "Jew" signifies.

What does it mean to be a "normal" Jewish family today? As we learn each others' stories we hear the challenges and joys of reconciling our sometimes competing identities of being Jewish while also feminist, Arab, gay, African-American, or Korean. We were a mixed multitude in ancient times, and we still are. May we continue to see the many faces of Israel as a gift that enriches our people.

Reprinted with permission from *Sh'ma: A Journal of Jewish Responsibility*, June 2003 <www.shma.com>.

Manasseh's Children

Michael Freund

The road to Aizawl winds perilously through lush green hills, with hairpin turns and narrow, unmarked lanes adding a tangible sense of danger to the journey. The route passes through numerous villages, many of which are essentially small clusters of makeshift homes built from bamboo, wood, and whatever else is available.

After a long and tiring journey, a van carrying four Israeli rabbis pulls into the town, which is the capital of the northeastern Indian state of Mizoram. The visitors stand before a building whose metal roof is crowned by a sign reading *"Shalom Tzion Beit Knesset."* Dozens of men wearing kippot and tzitzit and women wearing long sleeves and head-coverings gather at the entrance, greeting the delegation with Hebrew songs and hearty cries of "Shalom." Many have tears in their eyes as they wave Israeli flags briskly in the air.

The Israeli team, consisting of Efrat Chief Rabbi Shlomo Riskin, Rabbi Eliyahu Birnbaum of the Chief Rabbinate, Rabbi Eliyahu Avihail of the Amishav organization, and his son Rabbi David Avihail of Mitzpe Ramon, are clearly touched by the scene. After all, they are being welcomed by the Bnei Menashe, a group that claims descent from one of the 10 Lost Tribes of Israel.

About 4,500 Bnei Menashe live in towns and villages scattered throughout the Indian states of Mizoram and Manipur, with a handful in Assam and Myanmar as well. Members of the Mizo and Kuki tribes, they have passed down through the generations the tradition that they are descendants of the lost tribe of Manasseh, which was exiled from the Land of Israel by the Assyrians in 723 BCE.

A century ago, when British missionaries entered the region, they were astonished to find that the local tribesmen worshipped one God and were familiar with many of the stories of the Bible. Before long, the missionaries managed to convert most of Mizoram's population. Yet many of them, Christians and other tribesmen alike, continue to preserve the belief that they are descended from the ancient Israelites.

A little over 25 years ago, a group of Bnei Menashe decided to return to Judaism. They began building synagogues and *mikvaot* (ritual baths), and undertook to live in accordance with Jewish law. Shortly thereafter, an Indian Jew living in Israel passed along a letter from the Bnei Menashe to Rabbi Eliyahu Avihail of Jerusalem, who seeks out and assists "lost Jews." As founder and director of Amishav (literally "My People Returns"), Rabbi Avihail has since been to India six times to investigate the Bnei Menashe. He is convinced of the authenticity of their traditions.

"As I studied the community and learned about its ancient beliefs, I could not help but conclude that they are in fact descended from the tribe of Menashe," says Rabbi Avihail. "They have ancient songs and chants with words from the

Bible. For centuries, their children have been taught to sing *Litenten Zion*, which means Let us go to Zion, even though they had no idea what Zion was." Rabbi Avihail was especially intrigued to learn of Bnei Menashe customs such as laws of family purity, the use of a lunar calendar, and mourning rites—many of which bear a striking resemblance to those in the Bible. "There is simply too much similarity between their customs and ours for it to be coincidental," he said.

In the past decade, Rabbi Avihail has brought some 700 Bnei Menashe to Israel, with the approval of the Interior Ministry and the Chief Rabbinate. Recently he was back in India to introduce his colleagues, Rabbi Riskin and Rabbi Birnbaum, to the community.

After entering the synagogue in Aizawl, the rabbis join the 100-odd worshipers in afternoon prayer, led in fluent Hebrew by the Bnei Menashe's chief cantor, Eliezer Sela. Sela, a father of nine, has seven children living in Israel, each of whom has undergone formal conversion. "I cannot wait to go to Israel, the land of my forefathers," Sela says, adding, "we pray for its well-being every day."

At the end of the prayer service, Rabbi Riskin and Rabbi Avihail address the community, emphasizing the importance of adhering to Jewish law and studying the Torah. Rabbi Riskin speaks emotionally about the need to have faith in God's promise of redemption, and he captures his listeners' hearts by telling them, in the local Mizo dialect, "You are my brothers and sisters."

To locals living in Mizoram, there is no question about the origins of the Bnei Menashe. Lal Thlamuana, 45, a devout Christian who is the proprietor and principal of the local Home Mission School, has no doubt about the Israelite origins of the Mizo people. Thlamuana is a member of Aizawl's elite, speaks fluent English, has traveled abroad, and lives in a grand home brimming with servants. "Even Christian Mizos believe that we are descendants of Israel," he says, and proceeds to expound on a number of the community's ancient customs and traditions, such as circumcision of newborn boys on the eighth day, levirate marriage, and strict laws regarding menstruation, all of which are strikingly similar to Jewish law.

The British, Thlamuana notes, referred to the Mizo people as *Lushei*, a mispronunciation of *Lu Se*, which means "Ten Tribes" in the language of neighboring Burma. According to the Bnei Menashe, their ancestors migrated south from China to escape persecution, settling in Burma and then moving westward into what is now Mizoram and Manipur in India.

A sampling of Christian Mizos throughout Aizawl seemed to verify Thlamuana's assertion. Shopkeepers, airport workers, and others, when asked about the origins of the Mizo people, all respond with the same answer: "We are from the Israelites." Mr. Ropianga, a polished receptionist at the government-run tourist lodge in Aizawl, replies matter-of-factly, "Yes, of course we are descended from Israel. Everyone knows this." Though a practicing Christian, he was visibly moved when handed a postcard bearing an Israeli flag.

Driving through the streets of Aizawl, it is evident that there is a great deal of identification and support for Israel among the general populace. The main market is located on a thoroughfare called Zion Street, and many shops have names such as "Jewish Store" and "Israel Warehouse," none of which are owned by Jews.

While in Mizoram, Rabbi Riskin and his colleagues met with Mr. F. Malsawma, Mizoram's state minister of law. A devoutly religious Christian, the minister was more than happy to discuss the issue of the Mizos' Israelite descent. "We have a sentimental attachment to Israel, by blood also," he said, noting that "We claim to be Israelites—even our church leaders agree."

Malsawma told the rabbis that the government of Mizoram was researching the link between the Mizos and the Jews. "We are in the process of doing the research to see if we are descended from Menashe. Time will reveal the truth." The meeting between the rabbis and the minister led off the local television news that evening.

As part of their visit, Rabbi Riskin and his colleagues also spoke with a large number of people from the Bnei Menashe community itself. One of them, Yossi Hualngo, a 65-year-old resident of Aizawl, provided a key piece of the puzzle. Two of his father's brothers were priests who conducted the ancient Mizo rituals prior to the arrival of the Christian missionaries a century ago. Hualngo, speaking through an interpreter, offered a detailed description of the Mizo rites recounted to him decades ago by his uncles. As Rabbi Riskin noted, the similarities with Jewish ritual are startling.

According to Hualngo, his uncles would don white garments before carrying out sacrificial rites, including one with strings dangling from its four corners, reminiscent of the tallit with *arba kanfot* (the four-cornered ritual prayer shawl) worn by Jews. In the spring, an animal would be slaughtered and offered up as a sacrifice, and its blood smeared on the doorways of people's homes, suggesting the ancient Passover rite. Indeed, according to Hualngo, there was a rule that the Mizo priests had to carefully remove the meat from the bones of the animal without breaking any of them, just as Jewish law requires.

Then, in a remarkable scene, Hualngo proceeds to chant one of the incantations that his uncles had told him they used to sing while conducting important sacrificial ceremonies. The words in the song, and their biblical origin, are unmistakable: Terah, Abraham, Isaac, Jacob, the Red Sea, Marah and Shiloh (site of the ancient tabernacle and capital of the Twelve Tribes of Israel until the Assyrian conquest). Those present, Rabbi Riskin included, are stunned. "If anyone doubts the tremendous power of the Jewish soul, if anyone questions the magnificent strength of Jewish traditions, if anyone for one moment would question the eternity of the Jewish people, this proves its strength," Rabbi Riskin says.

"For me, it is surrealistic. I look around, I am in India, near the Burmese border, with tremendous poverty all around me, and here are what appear to be contented Jews living a very Jewish life and having one real hope and dream: to come to Israel as soon as possible and rejoin their people. It is the miracle of Jewish survival," he says.

Among the leading proponents of the theory that the Mizos are descendants of Israel is a local Christian scholar, Mrs. Zaithanchhungi, whose husband is a member of parliament. "Many people believe the Mizos are descended from Menashe," she says, adding, "I didn't believe it at first, but I went throughout Mizoram and spoke to village elders and collected ancient traditions and folklore." She has written a book, *Israel-Mizo Identity*, which details Mizo customs and compares them with Jewish tradition. Before the advent of Christianity in the area, Zaithanchhungi writes, "the Mizos believed in one Almighty God, the Creator of all things." At family sacrificial ceremonies, they would chant, "God above, we the sons of Menashe offer you the blood of an animal."

She also quotes an ancient song sung by the Mizos on special occasions, which parallels the biblical account of the Jews' Exodus from Egypt: "We had to cross the Red Sea, our enemies were coming after us with chariots, the Sea swallowed them all, as if they are meat. We are led by the cloud during the day, and by fire at night. Take those birds for the food, and drink water coming out from the rock."

While in Mizoram, the rabbis visited Bnei Menashe communities outside Aizawl as well, including synagogues in the villages of Vairengte, Kolasib, and Sihphir. In each township, they joined local communities in prayer and study, praising their commitment to Judaism and urging them to learn more about their heritage. After spending three days in Mizoram, the delegation proceeded to the neighboring state of Manipur, where the bulk of the Bnei Menashe live.

Upon arrival in Imphal, the capital of Manipur, the rabbis are taken straight from the airport to a large theater, where over 500 Bnei Menashe have gathered to greet them. The rabbis are presented with flowers, and community dignitaries express hope that the community will soon be allowed to immigrate to Israel.

Manipur itself is a politically unstable region that is home to dozens of underground groups fighting the government. Elections being held contribute to the tension, and the streets of the capital are filled with armed soldiers and policemen in riot gear. Violent protests and riots have recently taken place, though all appears quiet during the rabbis' stay.

Over Shabbat, Rabbi Riskin and the rest of the Israeli delegation stay at Amishav House, a community center and synagogue built by Rabbi Avihail on behalf of the Bnei Menashe. Shabbat services are held, complete with a great deal of singing and dancing.

Rabbi Riskin describes it as one of the most invigorating Shabbats he has ever had. "To see 500 people in a synagogue on Shabbat in Imphal, Manipur, praying with all their hearts, and reading Hebrew and singing magnificent songs—it was just an amazingly inspiring experience."

On Shabbat, the community comes together for a celebration as the nephew of Bnei Menashe Council general-secretary Lemuel Haokip undergoes circumcision. The ceremony is performed by one of the community's two *mohels* (ritual circumcisers) and the boy is given the Hebrew name Shimon. Afterwards, the child's proud uncle delivers a lesson on Israel's covenantal relationship with God.

Prior to their return to Israel, the rabbis visit Churachandpur near the Burmese border, where the local Bnei Menashe community is completing construction of its third synagogue. Hundreds of men and women turn out and Rabbi Riskin offers a modest donation for the project.

Asked later whether he believes the Bnei Menashe are indeed descendants of a lost tribe of Israel, Rabbi Riskin says he "was very skeptical about the Lost Ten Tribes... the notion of the Lost Tribes and bringing the Lost Ten Tribes back to Israel always had for me an almost fairy-tale kind of aspect." However, his visit to India seems to have altered his view.

"I have now become convinced from listening to the stories that they record from their grandparents about the ancient customs, and from the fact that their Christian neighbors recognize that they too come from that same background. The fact is, it is very difficult not to accept their traditions that they come from the tribe of Menashe," Rabbi Riskin says. "The Bnei Menashe have maintained fundamental ceremonies and practices of Judaism for what seems to be thousands of years, despite the fact that they have been cut off appreciably from the rest of the Jewish people."

Summarizing his impressions of the Bnei Menashe, Rabbi Riskin says, "They have tremendous commitment, a tremendous sense of sacrifice, and tremendous love for Judaism and for the State of Israel. I can't think of better future citizens for our country."

Those sentiments are sure to bring a smile to the face of Lemuel Haokip and his fellow Bnei Menashe, all of whom are longing to come to Israel. As a child, Haokip recalls that on special occasions, such as a lunar or solar eclipse or upon feeling the tremors of an earthquake, his father would rush out of their home, gaze toward heaven and declare: "The Children of Menashe still live! The Children of Menashe still live!" And so, it seems, they do.

This article originally appeared in *The Jerusalem Post Magazine* of March 27, 2002.

A Visit to the Cochin Synagogue

Emma Kimor

On our way to a conference in Japan in 1970, my husband had us stop in Cochin, a city on the Malabar Coast of the state of Kerala in southwest India. It was his express intent that I, too, visit the famous Cochin synagogue and meet the members of the Jewish communities with whom he had made friends on three earlier visits.

They were all still there (this was before the majority had emigrated to Israel) and most hospitable, vying with each other to entertain us at their home for a special, usually spicy dinner—the Koders, the Cohens, the Haleguas, the Robys, as well as the Ben Eliyahus from the mainland. I don't quite remember who lent me the *lungi*—the daily women's wear consisting of a short, sleeveless satin blouse with a flower pattern and a plain, wrap-around ankle-length skirt—to keep me dressed until Indian Airlines got our suitcases back from wherever they had gone.

When did the Jews arrive in that lush land of pepper trees, ginger and cardamon, peacocks and picturesque Chinese fishing nets? Perhaps they came as traders of spices, ivory, teak and peacocks as far back as King Solomon's fleet. Or they came with the Romans in the 1st century CE, or as refugees after the destruction of the first Temple or second Temple. Mention of Jewish settlers in this region is found in the records of famous world travelers like Benjamin of Tudela, who wrote *Sefer ha-Massa'ot*, or *Book of Travels* in Hebrew in the 1160s; Italian Marco Polo (1254-1324); and Spaniard Vasco de Gama. De Gama died in Cochin on Christmas eve 1524, and was buried in the St. Francis Church right next to the Jewish community leader's house—the Koder House. When he landed in 52 CE, the apostle St. Thomas is said to have been received by a Jewish flute girl.

Another document, deemed to be "the most important work for the study of the history of the Jews of Cochin" (S.S. Koder), is the *Notisias Dos Judeos de Cochin*, 150 copies of which were published in Amsterdam in 1686. In it, Mosseh Pareyra de Paeva, one of four Jews sent by the Jewish community of Amsterdam to enquire about and report on the state of the community in Cochin, gives a full account. The copious information they gathered includes the places from which each family had come: Jerusalem, Turkey, Persia, Syria, Palestine, Germany and Spain, as well as Cranganore—the port they eventually had to relinquish.

Whenever and however the Jews may have arrived, it is important to understand that they were most liberally received by the local reigning

122

maharajahs. Privileges and grants were accorded them such as those enjoyed only by the highest Indian dignitaries. The very first record of such a grant is a pair of copper plates, proudly and zealously preserved in the synagogue. Dated 379 CE, the grant of all princely rights of the Kingdom of Anjuvannam at the port of Cranganore (or Shingly, as this important international trading outlet was then called) is handed to the Jewish community leader Joseph Rabban as a hereditary possession for "so long as the world and moon exist."

However, this autonomous Jewish realm, in which they flourished as merchants, financiers, landowners, and courtiers, was not to survive as long as the world and moon exist. In 1567 invading Moors and Portuguese drove the Jews to abandon their Eden. But they found haven in nearby Cochin, which proved to be another Eden. The now-famous synagogue was built there in 1568 by the newcomers—four pious Jews named Samuel Castiel, David Belelia, Ephraim Salla and Joseph.

To say that I was awed by the magnificence of the synagogue is an understatement. In 1970, two years after its 400th anniversary celebrations, the synagogue was honored by the presence of then Prime Minister Indira Ghandi, and declared a part of the national Indian heritage. It is at the end of "Jew Town," built on the very palace grounds afforded the Jews by a benevolent maharajah, next to a Hindu temple where rajahs are crowned. Even viewed from afar, the Paradeshi Synagogue stands out with its square bell tower and clock with Hebrew, Malayalam, and Roman numerals. (Malayalam is the language used by the population of Kerala, containing some Tamil and Sanskrit words.) The name Paradeshi, Pardesi, Parthesi or Faradesi, (from the old Malayalam and Sanskrit *parthesis*), indicates "built by foreigners." It was first built in 1568, partially wrecked by the invading Portuguese, and rebuilt in 1664 with the aid of the Dutch, who had captured Cochin and were favorable to the Jews. The clock tower was added in 1761, and the unique Chinese tiling was added the year after. This historic landmark, this "Taj Mahal of the Indian Jews," as an American scholar has called it, may thus in many ways be said to symbolize the saga of the Jewish experience on the Malabar Coast.

Entering the synagogue, with its 12 windows (for the 12 tribes), what impressed me most is difficult to say. The glittering chandeliers? The two pillars bearing the names of Yachin and Boaz, supporting the upper bimah (pulpit) that was used for Torah, Shabbat, and festival services? The second bimah in the center of the synagogue for ordinary prayers? (Such double pulpits are a characteristic feature of Kerala synagogues.) I might also mention the valuable gifts presented to the synagogue: a golden crown for the Torah presented by a Maharajah of Travancore and two silver lamps from a British colonel, as well as many others presented by other Jews.

I was particularly enchanted by the story of the beautiful, hand-painted, no-two-identical tiles with a rare blue-on-white willow pattern—ordered by the maharajah for his palace from Canton, China. When they arrived and he learned that the dye contained cow's blood, he could not use them—the cow being sacred in Hindu belief. He was relieved when a rich merchant Jew, Ezekiel Rahabi, offered to buy them and presented them to the fortunate synagogue.

Sadly, all this splendor has become but a lonely landmark at present, doomed as a national heritage not to be moved, while most of the Jewish communities are gone. Still it is the only Kerala synagogue that holds services, relying on some Jews among the hundreds of tourists visiting daily to fill in the minyan (minimum of ten Jewish men needed for congregational prayer.) In 1997 it was graced by the visit of Queen Elizabeth II.

My husband would tell me about his very first visit, back in the 1960s. As their guest on Simchat Torah, he described to me how the dignitaries, holding the heavy scrolls in their arms, would circle the synagogue building, dancing and chanting, and get into such ecstasy that they would jump up with the scrolls "meters high."

Years later, as Simchat Torah guests of a Cochin family living at Rehasim, not far from Haifa, I was disappointed not to see them jump up, in no way ecstatic, as I had expected finally to see with my own eyes what my husband had witnessed in India. I asked why and was answered that the ecstasy in the *Golah* (Diaspora) was an expression of their yearning for Zion—the same yearning that had brought them to the Holy Land of Israel. They came not because of persecution or any such reason that had made other communities emigrate. It was their love of Zion that has made them come.

A Permanent Record in an Impermanent World

Xu Xin

Four hundred years had lapsed since the Jews arrived in Kaifeng. During this time, the community had become at home and comfortable in its new environment, learning the Chinese language and culture, gaining familiarity with Chinese customs and rites.

The Jews were prosperous, thriving in the favorable political and social climate provided by the city of Kaifeng. At the high point of their recorded history, around the year 1400, their number reached five thousand.

Unlike Jews living in anti-Semitic lands where laws forbade them to participate in politics, the civil service, and public affairs, here they were encouraged to fully engage themselves in the opportunities open to their neighbors. Like everyone else, they could enhance their social status by taking and passing the formidable imperial examinations. These exams were open to anyone; that is, anyone willing and able to devote the time and effort necessary for serious study of Confucianism and the Chinese classics. For many, this meant a lifetime of study. As an old Chinese saying goes: "One has to spend at least ten years below the window [studying] since a hundred years are needed to bring up a learned scholar."

Presented with such an opportunity, many Jews flocked to enroll in Chinese schools, studied diligently, and prepared themselves for the exams. Of course, the more time they spent learning Confucianism and the Chinese classics, the less time they devoted to Torah study.

As a result, many completely lost their knowledge of Hebrew. Since the Torah had not been translated into Chinese, they were no longer able to read the Law, even if they had the time and desire to do so. By and by, those who were determined to take up a political career abandoned Torah study and became ever more ignorant of the history of their people.

Meanwhile intermarriage between the Jews and their Chinese neighbors continued, and acculturation turned into assimilation. As they adapted to their new home, fewer and fewer evinced enthusiasm for attending synagogue, participating in prayer, or for recapturing their traditional way of life.

The community elders were concerned. They urged people to visit the synagogue and listen to the reading of the Law. But as more and more people lost any knowledge of Hebrew, the prayers were rendered meaningless.

What additional measures could be taken to prevent ethnic extinction? The problem, as the elders saw it, was no longer how to survive as individual Jews, but how to survive collectively, as a recognizably Jewish community. If a feeling of Jewishness was embedded deep in the Jewish soul, thrust there by the prophets, how could it be reawakened?

After much discussion, the elders agreed that one practical method to keep history alive was to make it readily available to all, especially later generations. They determined to preserve what was known of their history and heritage by inscribing it on large stone steles. This way nothing would be lost; the community's history and traditions would be in a permanent rather than an ephemeral, oral form, and would be available from generation to generation.

Some believed that the writing should be exclusively in Hebrew. They insisted that Hebrew, rather than any other language, was unique to their religion. "We want the work to be holy and in line with our tradition," they asserted.

But the majority believed that the writing should be done in Chinese to make it possible for everyone to read and comprehend. They argued that their community had been living in China for so many years that Chinese had already replaced Hebrew as their mother tongue and the daily language of their lives. If they wanted to make the inscribed history comprehensible to every member of the community, as well as to later generations, there was no other alternative. And they cited a valid precedent:

"We had the Septuagint in ancient times," they said. "It was because of the Septuagint translation that the Greek-speaking Jews of Alexandria, Egypt, did not forget our tradition, and that the rest of the world became aware of the culture of the Jews."

Once they agreed that Chinese was the language of choice, the next consideration was the appropriate content.

As this was essentially to be a history of their people, they started the text with Abraham, the forefather of the Jews, beginning with these words:

> Abraham, the patriarch who founded the religion of Israel, was of the nineteenth generation from Adam. From the creation of heaven and earth the patriarchs handed down the tradition that they received. They made no image, flattered no spirits and ghosts, and believed in no superstitions. Instead they believed that spirits and ghosts cannot help men, that idols cannot protect them, and that superstitions are useless. So Abraham meditated only upon heaven.
>
> Abraham gave them [the concepts of the Jewish faith] to Isaac, who gave them to Jacob, who gave them to the Twelve Tribes, who passed them on to Moses. Moses transmitted them to Aaron, who gave them to Joshua. Joshua transmitted them to Ezra. And from that time on the religion of the patriarchs glowed with renewed brilliance....

As to how Moses got the law, the Ten Commandments, it says:

> Intelligent, benevolent, and righteous, Moses sought the law on Mount Sinai, where he fasted for forty days and forty nights. His earnest prayers moved God's heart, and that is how the Torah, in

fifty-three sections, originated. *Meticulous and excellent, they inspire goodness in the good and expose the wickedness of the bad.*

Now it came to their history in China. They decided to write the following:

Our religion was transmitted to China from the west. We settled in Kaifeng by imperial command. More than seventy clans named Li, An, Ai, Gao, Mu, Zhao, Jin, Zhou, Zhang, Shi...arrived during the Northern Song Dynasty [960- 1127], bringing entry tribute of western cloth. The emperor said: "You have come to our Central Plain. Preserve yourancestral customs and settle in Biangliang [Kaifeng]."
In the first year of the Long Xing period [1163] of Song, when Chief Rabbi Levi was the leader of our faithful, the building of our synagogue was commenced....

During the Ming Dynasty [1368-1644] persons who were well versed in the Scriptures and urged others to do good were designated rabbis and elders. They preached our religion. Thanks to their efforts, today all of our people observe the law, worship God, venerate their ancestors, are loyal to their sovereign and filial to their parents.

The text continues with an account of the Jewish community's life in China.

This long inscription was carved on a special stone called the Number One Stele erected in the courtyard of the synagogue in 1489 so that everyone who came was able to read it.

Many years later, the Jews of Kaifeng, fearing that in time the story of their community would not be handed on, prepared a second stele providing further details of their life. This record has given the modern world valuable history about the life and times of these Jews. The great steles proved to be a treasure for historians, for while the synagogue was twice swept away by floods of the Yellow River, the monumental inscriptions were preserved. Later on people commented on this fortuitous circumstance, saying that it was a miracle brought about because God would not allow the name of His chosen people to perish.

For the present-day Jews of Kaifeng, descendants of the original settlers who are now integrated with the massive native Chinese population, the steles still serve as a substantive record of their heritage, silently retelling the history of their ancestors.

---

*The Torah is usually divided into 54 portions for weekly study and liturgical reading; the Kaifeng Jews divided it into 53 portions.

This story originally appeared in *Legends of the Chinese Jews of Kaifeng* by Xu Xin with Beverly Friend, (KTAV 19995).

Jews by Choice

Shir Teshuvah
(A Song of Turning)

W. Luther Jett

I tremble
when You call my name,
unworthy as I am
to hear, and still You call.
Though I am furtive,
I cannot hide my heart.

The sea will not divide
You from me, but parts
to deliver me naked
on the sand before You.

The desert will not make
itself my sanctuary,
but raises a mountain
to bring You closer.

I stop my ears
with the fingers of my hands,
but your Voice
moves my broken heart.

Until I cry out
from the darkness in which
I have swallowed my self.

And, where I am,
You hear;
shattered as I am,
You see.

Turning to that
which sees and hears,
the veil falls

from my eyes,
my ears are opened.

Out of the night,
I come to the day.
Out of wilderness,
I approach your gates.

You do not turn
me aside,
it was I who turned,
You who reclaim
that I might
re-turn to You
freely.

This poem was written for Rosh Hashanah 5753.

My Re-Invented Name

W. Luther Jett

An open hand beckoned me,
and I entered
a strange place that is home;
a simple song
I swear I never heard
before brought tears
of memory to my eyes.

How long did I wander?
Generations?
Unknowing and longing
to understand,
turning, at last, to find
I have returned.
As I hear, I am heard.

I was given a name,
but its meaning
was a mystery left
to be earned;
so, in strange letters, I
write it anew,
because out of darkness
I am awakened.

This poem was written for Rosh Hashanah 5754

Mikveh Surprise

Robin K. Levinson

It took almost a year to arrange our adopted son's official conversion to Judaism. We are liberal Jews but sought an Orthodox conversion so no one could ever accuse Aaron of being any "less Jewish" than we are. Having been born in Korea, Aaron will face enough obstacles as he embraces his Jewish identity. Why, we reasoned, should his form of conversion present one more potential obstacle? Aaron might want to immigrate to Israel someday. Who's to know whether the current non-recognition of Reform and Conservative conversions there will be a permanent fixture of Israeli life? So an Orthodox conversion it would be.

Luckily, my husband's family rabbi is an Orthodox rabbi, even though he is the spiritual leader of a Conservative temple—the same temple that my husband's family belonged to since he was a boy. The same temple that my in-laws supported generously for decades. The same rabbi who bar mitzvahed my husband and his siblings, and who officiated at the funeral of my husband's father 25 years ago. The same rabbi who officiated at my mother-in-law's wedding several years later and who also officiated at my wedding. It seemed natural that this same rabbi should be part of the *beit din* for Aaron's conversion.

So, there we were, sitting opposite three elderly Orthodox rabbis at a mikveh in North Jersey, a two-hour drive from home. As the video camera rolled, the rabbis began to ask questions.

Yes, we were planning to send Aaron to a Jewish preschool, the same school our biological daughter, Zoe, was attending. As if on cue, Zoe began singing, "Bim, Bam, Shabbat Shalom." We all erupted into laughter.

Are there Jewish symbols are in our home? Mezuzahs, Judaic art, Jewish spirituality books, menorahs, Shabbat candlesticks, haggadahs, a Seder plate. There were more than I had realized.

Did we belong to a temple? My husband quickly pointed out that I was a board member of a small, alternative congregation that had formed just a couple of years before. The rabbis seemed very impressed. I mentioned that I also attended a monthly women's Torah study group because I needed to educate myself in order to educate my children. The rabbis were impressed by this, too.

"What would it take to get you to join *my* shul?" one of them asked rhetorically.

"It's very important," the rabbi continued, "that Aaron be exposed to as many Jewish themes and rituals as possible from a very young age. This will help him build a strong core identity, one that will not waver if it is ever challenged by outside forces." I agreed wholeheartedly.

Finally, it was time for the ritual bath. I undressed Aaron. Zoe, not to be upstaged, stripped and was allowed to accompany her brother into the warm waters of the mikveh. The rabbis recited some prayers. My husband dunked Aaron and briefly let go so the water would touch every square inch of his golden skin. More prayers were uttered. We all sang, "*Mazel tov v'simchah tov...*"

Then something totally unexpected happened to me. I began to feel the presence of God in the room. It seemed surreal, almost electric, like the first time I touched the Western Wall. All my prior apprehensions about the conversion had morphed into the single most spiritual moment of my life. I couldn't be prouder for giving the world another Jew.

After the singing, I told the rabbis what an acquaintance had said when I mentioned we were going to convert Aaron to Judaism. "How can you impose your religion on another person who's too young to have a say in the matter?" the acquaintance had asked.

"This is not an imposition," I responded. "It's a gift."

Until Aaron's mikveh, I never realized the incredible gift his conversion would be to me, too.

Modern Israel

Jerusalem Again—January 2001*

Elaine Starkman

1
Jerusalem splinters and reinvents itself again.
More than a tangible city, it thrives
on "If I forget thee,"—
juggler, fortress, syndrome.

2
What you think is good is hateful to others.
Who can be right when the brilliant sun
sets beyond the wall and stray cats
snarl in this city unlike any other.

3
"Abundant love breaks through law;
embraced by the sheltering
mother of the world," Shira says.
"They don't think like us," says Tal.
"Ask the Christians who they want
guarding their holy sites, ask them."

4
The Arab cabbie starts his meter too soon.
My spouse won't enter his cab.
Under his breath the driver curses.
"It's just a few shekels," I shout.
"It's more than that," he answers,
and I know what he means.
I'm angry at my principled man.
He has one standard for all cabbies.
Soon we stand in a silent circle of anger,
the cabbie, my husband and me.

5
The Arab child hops over an unmarked
 line between her quarter and ours
in the *shuk.* She's learned
to beg for pennies. She's learned

how to draw buyers to her brother's shop.
He complains, "Jews won't
come here, they want us to starve."
I answer in a distant third person.
"They are not all that way,"
and buy a sun hat.
The child skips back and forth
between boundaries, the only one
not yet afraid.

*Third Prize Winner, 2002 Kulanu International Writing Competition.

This poem will appear in *MOVING: Poems 1992-2002* by Elaine Starkman.

170

Gila Green

Like yesterday's lesson: erased.
Like the map: can't be put right.
Exploded in the morning light.
Bodies shoot up.
Parts and parts of bodies.
Leap up apart.
170 beating hearts.
Spread far out.
Like human firecrackers.
Hold everyone.
Breathe and hold.
Today it drips in the City of Gold.

The sound must be like.
And the scene must look like.
And the ground must smell like.
The past.
Jews still tend to die en masse.

This is to say how much that hurts.
How their souls must have been snatched by surprise.
As the light burst through their eyes.
Pain like fingers in and out of an electric blade.
And then the toes.
And then the face.

How to say sorry: apologize.
For not saving your precious lives.
When you thought it was so safe.
To take the bus to work that day.
How to express you will be remembered.
Your deaths are not worth less.

In memory of all.
Who never got to be.
Prayers for mercy running deep.
Peace for the shattered.
The dead and the living.
Peace for the killed.
And for the killing.

This poem was written in 1995.

Upon Returning from a Trip to Israel

Lori Levy

How was your trip? they ask, puffing on cigarettes, stirring coffee,
poised at the other end of the telephone, more anxious, perhaps,
to share their news than to listen to mine.
It was good, is all I say,
good, meaning I lounged on a yellow beach chair,
seduced by the sun; frisked with friends in the waves
of the Mediterranean, laughing, always laughing—
on the same shore where a soldier, patrolling the Promenade,
sliced a garbage bag open to check for bombs.
Good, meaning the kissable cheeks of my nephew
as he bounced like a bright ball on the couch, behind my sister—
while we stared at the newspaper on the table,
at the remains of Sbarro Restaurant in Jerusalem, where a bomb
exploded, killing, among others, five members of a family
who drove into town that day for something as simple
as pizza and coke, and a break from war.
Good, meaning goose liver pate, fresh trout, desires stirred
by breezes at sunset on the balcony in Tel Aviv,
life going on amidst mortars and missiles,
drive-by shootings on the West Bank.
Good, I say, meaning yes, there's more,
but where do I start? And how?—when the story inside me
will only come out in the shape of a poem.

In Jerusalem Flowers

Lynn Schubert

And we must talk of them all,
the roots and the stems of us,
flowers that have fallen,
leaves reaching out into
a storm of winters like this
and all the rest of the seasoned
bitter and sweetness of being,
buried beneath the words,
the longing, these terrible eyes
that will not rest from
what they have ever seen
in Jerusalem flowers,
the bloody red
the yellow stars of us
the gorgeous blue

All of Us

By The Light

Rachel S. Epstein

Look in my window--
you can see us all whispering together
beneath the shadows of a flaming life.

Smiles lit by the glow of the menorah,
its beautiful power the center of
a family's love.

The colored flame shoots its glance
at each of us
individually.

We move in closer together
so we may be engulfed
at the same time.

We look at each other.

Even as the candles burn lower,
the wicks losing their strength,
we stand together.

Nobody speaks.

Nobody has to.

We are a family.

The Face of the Waters

Paul Wieder

At the beginning of the Beginning
You moved upon the face of the waters
At the beginning of our beginning
We lived in Your Garden between Your rivers

At the end of our beginning
You floated us above Your floods
And you promised our forefather
His children would number
As the sands of Your seas

You have always moved
On the face of our waters

At the birth of our great teacher,
You carried his cradle on the river
When we were told we could not be free to bless You,
You made the river cry tears of blood

As you brought us forth to our redemption,
You made watery walls of the surging sea
And You sustained us in the wilderness of sand
By turning a stone into a fountain

You have always moved
On the face of our waters

Now that we have wandered all Your oceans,
Now that we have wept oceans of tears,
Return us like the tides to the Great Sea,
And we will
Weave by the Sea of the Reed,
And eat by the Sea of the Salt,
And sing by the Sea of the Harp.

Until and beyond that day—

May You always move
On the face of our waters.

If It's Dark Out

Ruth Fogelman

If it's dark out,
Turn on the lights.
Turn up the music.
Turn around.
Look at all those people.
Look around.
What do you see?
What do you hear?

Seventy faces are lighting up.
Seventy tongues are clamoring to convey
The meaning of the ancient text.
Seventy faces of the diamond
Of the Divine Word.
Seventy rhythms beating simultaneously -
Each allowing the other space for its own interpretation.
Seventy instruments of the orchestra
Playing in harmony
The Divine Melody.

Kulanu

Music by Jerry Cooper
Lyrics by Jocelyn and Jerry Cooper

sing a song of our peo - ple

KU -LA - NU means e - ev - ery

one. Bro - thers and

sis - ters to geth - er our sto - ry goes

on and on.

Brothers and sisters kulanu,
Family wherever you go
My brother is white; he is yellow or brown
In tropical lands or in snow

CHORUS
We sing a song for our people
Kulanu means everyone
The tie that strengthens and binds us
The story goes on and on

Brothers and sisters kulanu
Links in our holy chain
History calls to us, future is there for us
Brothers we'll always remain

CHORUS